LYING AND LIE DETECTION
A CIA INSIDER'S GUIDE

JOHN G. KIRIAKOU

Skyhorse Publish

For Max

All Rights Reserved. No part of this book may be reproduced in any manner without the express written consent of the publisher, except in the case of brief excerpts in critical reviews or articles. All inquiries should be addressed to Skyhorse Publishing, 307 West 36th Street, 11th Floor, New York, NY 10018.

Skyhorse Publishing books may be purchased in bulk at special discounts for sales promotion, corporate gifts, fund-raising, or educational purposes. Special editions can also be created to specifications. For details, contact the Special Sales Department, Skyhorse Publishing, 307 West 36th Street, 11th Floor, New York, NY 10018 or info@skyhorsepublishing.com.

Skyhorse® and Skyhorse Publishing® are registered trademarks of Skyhorse Publishing, Inc.®, a Delaware corporation.

Visit our website at www.skyhorsepublishing.com.

10 9 8 7 6 5 4 3 2 1

Library of Congress Cataloging-in-Publication Data is available on file.

ISBN: 978-1-5107-5611-3
eBook ISBN: 978-1-5107-5614-4

Cover design by Kai Texel

Printed in the United States of America

Author's Note

Contents

Introduction

WHEN WE THINK OF LIES, IT'S obvious that they come in very different categories. Some of them entail tremendous financial losses for investors or even for those who have bought products that were of no value but carried a high price. Financial lies can be quantified and, thanks to modern investigatory procedures, they can be exposed. Other lies relate to personal matters. Breach of promise disputes illustrate the consequences of personal dishonesty and deception. Tabloid newspapers offer us numerous accounts of the "black widows" who have married elderly rich men in eager expectation of their early deaths. Some of those deaths are hastened by poisonous concoctions of the women who have married for money but lack the patience to wait. When this happens, there will often be a police investigation that will explore the many lies told in connection with these "love affairs." From the outright criminal we can proceed to the category of political lies. Their prevarications reveal the dishonest ambitions of politicians who are motivated by greed rather than a desire to serve the public. Sometimes they simply expose the politician who presents himself as the defender of family values as a philanderer using his exalted political position to exploit vulnerable women.

Who needs to detect lies? This is an important question. We might automatically think of police interrogators or counterintelligence officers. They obviously need to be able to separate the truth from the lies. More importantly, everyone needs to do this. In all of our interactions—whether dealing with a used car salesman, a suspicious spouse or a politician seeking our vote—we face this challenge. Throughout the day, people are demanding our attention and we have to filter out spurious or dishonest messages. Even if we are not paranoid, each day is punctuated by situations that demand our attention to possible lies or deceptions.

No discussion of the art of lying is complete without a consideration of political lies. Those lies range from blatant and shameless to surprisingly complete and hidden in rhetoric. Hannah Arendt, one of the most respected political philosophers of the 20th century, and the author of *Truth, Politics, and Lying*, speculated about the lies of politicians. According to Arendt, mendacity contributes to the development of the totalitarian state and totalitarian leaders secure the allegiance of their citizens through coercion and manipulation. Because of the pervasive nature of lies, it appears that most politicians are not interested in truth but simply in the acquisition of power. After the Watergate scandal and a nationwide obsession with President Richard Nixon's lies, candidate Jimmy Carter tried to walk around the edges of this issue. Carter proclaimed that he "would never knowingly lie" to the American people. That statement raised curious and confusing questions about what constitutes a lie. Does telling an untruth always constitute a lie or might it be evidence of one's stupidity? Or does it mean making a promise that turned out to be beyond possibility?

There are many reasons it is difficult to detect lies or deception in politics. One common reason stems from the failure to distinguish between a belief and a fact. If a politician expresses his belief that, for example, Mexico will pay for the border wall, that is a prediction. It may be incorrect, but it is not a lie. However, if a politician says Mexico already paid for the wall, that is a lie, since it references a fact that is not in evidence. In a similar vein, the now notorious promise of "if you like your health insurance plan, you can keep it" was revealed to be a lie rather than an inaccurate prediction. When it was spoken, the authors of the Affordable Care Act knew this was not going to happen. In the end, we are left with a popular association that most politicians and government officials routinely lie to us. Many people will refuse to read books written by politicians because they expect their accounts to either be self-serving or completely untruthful.

Political figures prefer to "spin" any story in a way that advances their interest. All too often "spin" simply means to lie or distort reality.

It is also difficult to detect a political lie because people are wedded to their identification with a particular political party. People will listen to statements made by someone affiliated with their political party and suspend all critical thinking. If the statement is not associated with a political party it might impinge on one of the "way of life" disputes such as abortion and, therefore, have religious implications. Something as easily verifiable as statistics about the topic may be automatically dismissed as a falsehood without even checking.

Closely related to this category of statement is the utilization of the so-called fact checker. There is an assumption that the fact checker is not only completely objective but, more importantly, is qualified to pass judgement on matters in a multitude of disciplines. This claim is rarely plausible and people who reverentially cite a fact checker as a reason for accepting or rejecting a statement of fact are using a fallacious method of determining truth. Even less plausible is the use of a fact checker to evaluate what is, in effect, merely opinion or an evaluation of a theoretical concept.

A discussion of lying must begin with a definition. Before working on the issue of how to determine if someone is lying, we need to know what constitutes a lie. The common definition of a lie is that it is a false statement made with the intent to deceive. This definition is extremely narrow. A better definition is that a lie is a statement made by someone who does not believe it, but who directs it at someone he hopes will believe it. The first definition is based on an assumption that the statement is actually false. The second one simply requires that the person who makes that statement does not believe it although he might be wrong and the statement could actually be true.

With this assumption, there are four basic requirements in identifying a lie. The first is that a statement is made, while the second requirement is that the person making the statement believes it to be false. The third is that the statement is addressed to another person. And the final requirement is that there is an intention that the addressee be persuaded to accept as true something that is not. The

relative complexity of this proposition fits in the world of psychological operations or deception and calls for an ability to recognize an elaborate or strategic lie. This is not the scenario in which an interrogator
stares into the face of a suspect trying to pick up a "tell" that might
indicate lying. Rather it ushers in the concept of strategic deception,
something which is on a significantly broader scale and likely more
consequential. The concept of propaganda must be considered when
evaluating psychological operations. There is an assumption that all
propaganda is untrue but the most effective propaganda is at least par-
tially true. It may be completely true, if actual facts are selected merely
because they prove a point.

A lie can be a simple misstatement of fact. It is an assertion that
something which is untrue is, in fact, true. A network of lies can help
in the development of a false narrative that constitutes deception. To
defeat a campaign of deception, it is essential to know if a person is
lying about specific issues. However, it may be that individual statements are true but through skillful manipulation of those facts, it is
possible to create a false narrative that is more damaging.

People often rationalize the telling of lies. They justify telling a lie
by explaining it as a way to avoid conflict that would be detrimental
to communal harmony. It is normal that you would not want to upset
people about whom you care. Others will admit that telling a lie is
simply a way to make a good impression. If you insist that your motives
are good, this can be presented as a step in accomplishing good things.
To do this you need to be seen as good, competent, or successful. In
short, lying is a way of avoiding the consequences of telling the truth.
But even in non-criminal settings, lying can undermine a relationship.
Once we enter the realm of criminal behavior, as will be seen below,
the consequences can be much more devastating.

The 4th Century BC Greek philosopher Diogenes is remembered
for his despair as he decried the state of popular honesty. In statues
he is portrayed carrying a lamp through the night in his futile search
to find an honest man. Throughout the Middle Ages and into the
Renaissance, scholars, priests, and philosophers speculated about the
dire state of public discourse being burdened with so many lies. Again

and again, they wrote that the world had never before faced such an epidemic of falsehoods. Among the European elite, men sought fortune and practiced every form of deception in order to acquire it. Modern studies indicate that lying is ubiquitous, with each person telling no fewer than ten lies each day and perhaps as many as a hundred. Regardless of the validity of such research, there is no doubt that we have to be on guard to protect ourselves from lies.

Lying has become a regular feature of most peoples' lives. Not surprisingly, lying has even become a form of popular entertainment. A popular show called *Pretty Little Liars* is a series about four teenagers who band together in an effort to expose the person responsible for the disappearance of their friend. The program routinely features effective tactics for telling or exposing lies. A British thriller television series entitled "Liar" is the story of a teacher in the middle of a breakup who is set up on a date with a doctor. The dramatic complications begin as viewers attempt to sort out the deceptions and lies told when the teacher accuses the doctor of raping her. Many television game shows are based on the abilities of contestants to identify the person who is telling lies. A brief search reveals a multitude of games such as Dr. Phil's "Liars Exposed on TV," Entertainment Daily's "People Caught Lying," or "Biggest Liars Caught on Camera." Since so many people fantasize about getting revenge against liars, it is not surprising that there is a show entitled "Liars Called Out." An outsider studying our culture would be inclined toward the assumption that lying is so common, that it must be generally acceptable.

In 2009 a movie entitled "The Invention of Lying" toyed with the concept of an alternative reality in which there was no such thing as lying. The central character is a screenwriter named Mark Bellison whose work is not very popular since there is no such thing as fiction. Fiction, after all, is founded on lies that do not yet exist. Not surprisingly, Mark loses his job and cannot pay his rent. Facing eviction, he goes to his bank to withdraw his remaining funds, $300. When the bank teller says their computers are down, she asks him how much money he has in his account. At this time, he has an epiphany and tells her he has $800, the amount needed to pay his rent. Having thus told the world's first lie, he proceeds to lie in other circumstances. The result, as developed in the plot, is that telling lies emerges as a way to actually help people. Mark introduces the concept of heaven, becomes wealthy, and becomes happily married to the woman of his dreams. The abundance of programs such as this, based heavily on the telling of lies, certainly encourages the acceptance of lies as part of popular culture.

Any person who has had the experience of giving testimony in court is not likely to realize that there was once a debate within the Christian community about the morality of lying. St. Augustine, at the age of 41, was appointed the Bishop of Hippo from 396 and held this position until his death in 430. He is regarded as the most profound of Christian thinkers and prolific Christian writers after St. Paul. His works, which have survived until today, considered the question of lying. He embraced the notion of a well-meant charitable lie and argued that excessive honesty could be just as destructive as a lie.

Much later secular writers defended courtly deceit and argued that lies were often necessary not only for one's survival but also in defense of the state itself. By contrast, theologians maintained that there could be no civil society unless people were able to work on the assumption of truthfulness and honesty. In response, members of the European courts saw lies as the only way to maintain social cohesion.

Going beyond the philosophical questions about the morality of lying, there are important practical issues to consider. If you are an intelligence analyst, for example, you have to evaluate concepts that are political or which impinge on the security of your state. If you are a businessman, your challenge is to look a person in the face and decide if that person is sincere. If you misread the signals in this communication, you may well lose money because of your failure to detect dishonesty. In a similar fashion, the individual who suspects a spouse of cheating is caught up in a personal dilemma which can become even worse because of a failure to identify when the other person is not honest.

Your ability to detect when a person is lying will be dependent on the method of communication. It is easier if the untruths are expressed in words. Most communication uses spoken or written words that can be examined directly. However, communication can also be expressed in physical gestures or in some physical movement. Most cultures recognize that a person who nods his head means that as an affirmative response. In effect, that is as good as the spoken word. An exclamation or a laugh can be misunderstood but it nonetheless is a method of deceit. The World War II spy Virginia Hall was successful because she knew how to disguise herself in a fashion that deceived German intelligence authorities. She dressed as an elderly French milkmaid who shuffled in order to hide her distinctive limp caused by her wooden leg. Because she looked innocuous and unimportant, she was never arrested by the Germans who were conducting an intensive search for her.

The case of Virginia Hall is significant because it underscores the need to be able to detect lies. During World War II, the Gestapo and other German intelligence organizations were known for their ability to break any story that might be told by an Allied spy or a domestic dissident. While the Nazis were noted for their brutal methods of torture, methods which they seemed to enjoy, a serious interrogation effort must be much more sophisticated. Whether working for a totalitarian dictatorship or for a presumably respectable state, it is important for an interrogator to be able to break the story or legend of a spy or a criminal.

A final concern is to determine who is responsible for the detection of a lie. The answer to that question depends on the nature of the lie. Is it associated with a criminal endeavor to steal cash from an institution? There are specialized police services that are related to specific types of crimes and officers in those services are trained to look for certain falsehoods. If there is an investigation of a murder or a robbery, there will be certain officers qualified to work on those cases. When the crime is a matter of national security, there is an entirely different skill set needed for the investigation. This is more complicated than simple theft and therefore presents different issues and concerns. The basic assumption is that different kinds of lies require different kinds of interrogation skills.

Lying and Lie Detection

Given the number of scams being perpetrated today, each individual faces a challenge in assessing the honesty of people who may approach him. As individuals, they lack the training offered to law enforcement professionals. For people who are looking for job opportunities on the Internet, it is vital that they be vigilant in examining each proposal. It is estimated that 97% of Internet based offers are fraudulent and desperate people are exceptionally vulnerable. Many job "offers" begin with a request for the applicant to pay a fee before he begins work and such a request is a clue that the offer is not legitimate. Most people have probably been informed in an email that they have won some tremendous prize but need to pay a fee before receiving that fortune. Of course, the lucky individual sends his money to the scam artist and never hears from him again.

Clarity of Simple Lies

LIES ARE NOT ALWAYS STRAIGHTFORWARD. Unlike the blithe assurances of fact-checkers, there is more to the determination of lies than just a mere fact. While lies are significant in terms of their use, the more important concern is that they are part of a process of misleading people. An encyclopedia or the Internet can answer basic questions such as the year in which the Treaty of Westphalia was signed. That is a simple matter. What matters is not that you can detect a simple lie but can you see through a lie that has an important, strategic value.

What lacks clarity if is issues relating to values, impressions, or feelings are comprised. Looking at strategic psychological operations, one sees the role of deception. Every fact used in the PSYOP campaign may be true, but are those facts actually relevant? Investigating a murder case will require a detective to check on the alibi of a suspect or on a number of facts. However, evaluating an advertisement requires much more work. There was a time when advertisements for cigarettes depended on a presentation of charming and smart looking people smoking them. The advertisement presents a pleasant image but nothing more. The cigarette is associated with prosperous people having a good time. They might be standing in an open field with scenic views of mountains. The advertisement may be misleading but it does not contain lies.

An ad campaign may be deceptive, but to see the deception requires the analyst to consider values. No fact checker can do this for you. It involves a logical process that can be extremely complicated. We think about how to detect a lie but this does not always show the deceptive pattern. Nor does it reveal the intentions of the government that has undertaken a PSYOP campaign against you. As can be seen in evaluating the World War II's Operation Mincemeat, the analyst needs to make a judgement about the adversary's intentions. In 1943, the planners of Operation Mincemeat wanted to convince the Germans to take certain military actions, actions that were beneficial to the Allies.

The old television detective show "Dragnet" showed Joe Friday repeatedly making the statement to witnesses "just the facts, ma'am." This request implies that facts tell the whole story when, in fact, the more important issue might be which facts are selected in telling the story. Each person will operate on the basis of perceptions and values that determine which facts are selected because they seem relevant to the question at hand. During the Cold War, many Westerners who were pro-Soviet visited Moscow. Their accounts of their visit would mention cheap rent, the low cost of the subway, and the apparent absence of inflation as things that impressed them. By contrast, anti-Soviet visitors noticed travel restrictions for Soviet citizens, the lack of a free press, and the restrictions on religious speech. For them, the relevant facts were those which underlined the oppressive features of the regime. All of their reports were factually accurate but it was the values of the tourists that determined what they saw as important features of the system.

The Need for Simple Lies

IN OUR EFFORT TO DISCERN THE truth behind lies, few things exceed the growing phenomenon of the fact checkers. These entities promise to protect us from the dreaded fake news that spreads disinformation. The fact checker promise is to expose the many untruths being peddled by politicians and others who expound on controversial public issues. In general terms, the fact checker concept is based on the assumption that lies will be simple matters of fact rather than complex issues requiring detailed, sophisticated research.

In 2016 Donald Trump said that 33% of would-be immigrant women heading north toward the US border had been subjected to sexual assault. He was pointing out the dangers of this journey. Fact checkers labeled his statement as "false" when a Doctors Without Borders report stated that 31% of the women had been assaulted. By itself, the 2% difference is minimal but it is more important to note that the Doctors Without Borders report was not the only data. It was convenient, so the fact checkers used it. There were, however, other agencies and entities, such as The New York Times, providing data that was even higher than 33%. Having different data providers is convenient but does not offer the certainty promised by fact checker advocates. People look to them for truth, but often they simply bring more confusion.

The work of fact checkers is ratified by the International Fact Checking Network (IFCN). IFCN is a worldwide forum for fact checkers and is hosted by a non-profit journalism school and research organization in Florida known as the Poynter Institute for Media Studies. Its work is based on a list compiled by the Southern Poverty Law Center that identified over 500 news sites deemed to be "unreliable." This list became a controversial issue and eventually Poynter had to discard the list when critics charged that conservative outlets were routinely disparaged on it. Importantly, the Poynter Institute owns the *Tampa Bay Times* as well as the International Fact Checking Network.

The first fact checking operation to enjoy success was Snopes. com, which was founded in 1993 by the husband and wife team of David and Barbara Mikkelson. It was intended to be an urban folklore website focused on urban legends. It expanded to cover more topics and relied on user discussions to determine the truth or falsity of stories. When Barbara stopped writing for the site and their work load increased, they hired people who had been submitting to the site's message board. Snopes came to enjoy widespread acceptance and, at one point, there was an effort to transform it into a television program. The site counts at least seven million visits each month. Because of its commercial success, ownership of the site became a legal controversy that has yet to be fully resolved. In 2019, Snopes expanded by purchasing another website known as OnTheIssues.org that serves as a vehicle for informing voters about various policy issues.

Over the past decade, fact checking has become a worldwide phenomenon, and it is especially relevant in Europe and Latin America. On 2 April 2017, the first International Fact Checking holiday was celebrated. This was an international effort to develop skills for identification of fake news and the protection of people from the effects of misinformation. Organizers for the event solicited fact checking resource materials from media outlets and encouraged the posting of articles on the importance of fact checking. The targets of these events were students, as well as the general public.

In spite of a growing international presence, the United States remains the world leader in its dependence on fact checking sites. Unfortunately, the proliferation of fact checking services has undermined their value because of the disparity of results. It is likely that this disparity is an understandable consequence of the complexity of issues and the difficulty of reducing answers to simple facts.

This difficulty was highlighted by the legal battle between Snopes and the satirical online publication *The Babylon Bee*. In 2018, an article joking that CNN used an industrial sized washing machine to spin the news appeared in *The Babylon Bee*. Snopes, in a fact check report, claimed that the obviously satirical article was false, a claim that prompted Facebook to threaten to de-platform the *Bee*. This embarrassing incident highlighted the shortcomings of the fact checking concept and led to apologies from both Snopes and Facebook.

In an effort to improve the methodological legitimacy of fact checking sites, computer specialists have worked on an algorithm for the identification of fake news. The algorithm is based on the appearance of certain words and symbols as well as of common word patterns. This approach is consistent with the efforts of graduate schools to improve the image of political science as a science in the fashion of disciplines like biology and physics. Because fact checking often suffers from negative popular perceptions, its proponents want to refute accusations that these sites are biased. In a 2016 Rasmussen survey, only 29% of the respondents indicated they trusted the process, while 62% did not. Defenders of the process complain that phony fact checking sites have been created, largely by Russia and Turkey, as part of a misinformation campaign against fact checkers.

Many of the issues faced by fact checking operations are obvious. Everyone makes mistakes, and working on such a diverse range of topics makes that inevitable when facing the true or false dichotomy. If new information comes in, a rating may change from "false" to "mixture" or even "true." The decisions are being made by reporters forced to evaluate issues about which they have no special expertise. In the end, they make pseudoscientific judgments on topics that relate to values and concepts, rather than to questions of specific fact.

The greatest utility of the fact checker may be in the area of non-controversial editorial matters. The fact checker staff of a magazine was responsible for determining the correct spellings of names, the verification of facts, such as dates of birth, and other matters that were important to publications. Fact checking opinions is not only much more difficult than checking specific facts, it is in many ways impossible.

In the search for truth, it is reckless to rely upon a fact checking organization when you can never be sure about the qualifications of the checkers. Nor can you be certain if those people have a particular political bias. It is one of those times when you are required to do your own research rather than outsource it to an unknown entity.

The widespread use of the term "deception" tells us that simple lies are a luxury too often not available in the marketplace of dishonesty. The head of East Germany's foreign intelligence service, Markus Wolf, wrote about his work in a book entitled *The Art of Deception*. In one example, he presents a clear picture of the necessary lack of clarity in his efforts to undermine Western intelligence services. Wolf describes a real life situation in which there are two Soviet defectors telling contradictory stories about Soviet involvement with Lee Harvey Oswald. The challenge for the security service is to weigh an abundance of often confusing information in order to decide which defector is truthful.

Liars in History

THERE IS ALWAYS SPECULATION ABOUT WHO are the most notorious liars in history. Such speculation has an important value in what it teaches us about the impact of lies as well as how to detect lies. Of course, if you are in the dentist's waiting room, you will often find popular magazines offering articles with titillating titles about America's most famous liars. These tend to be celebrities who have lied about their date of birth or who they may be dating. These lies are about trivial matters, unlike those that have to be unraveled by detectives or intelligence officers. Criminal, military, and economic disasters have been made possible because a person or a government has advanced lies about serious topics. The lies of an adolescent entertainer are of little consequence beyond offering a distraction for the fearful person waiting to see his dentist.

Historical records show that some of the most unlikely figures have advanced their careers through lies and deception. The record of Pope Alexander VI, who was born as Rodrigo de Borja and became pope in 1492, demonstrates that someone who is regarded as a successful pope could rise to prominence and power through unethical behavior. Before becoming pope, he amassed a considerable personal fortune and lived as a prince. Pope Alexander VI managed to secure important clerical leadership positions for his children and was known more for political intrigue than for spiritual teachings. He not only loved power but he also loved women and had several children by different women. His corruption and his neglect of spiritual teaching contributed to the revolt against the clerical elite. The result was the Protestant Reformation.

Even the so-called "Father of History," Herodotus, is associated with an impressive record of lies. Herodotus was a Greek writer and geographer whose influence on Western civilization is unparalleled. He was the product of a family of wealthy Greek merchants. His writing skill is proof of the quality of his education. Herodotus is noted for his unabashed tendency to embellish the truth or to even write complete distortions of what actually happened. His account of the Battle of Marathon, especially his identification of the families that were to get credit for this victory, was especially controversial. Much of his writing recounted things he had seen as he traveled. One claim for which he is remembered is that he saw ants in Persia that were the size of foxes and spread gold dust as they dug in the ground. This story was long cited as evidence of his dishonesty, although in 1984 a French explorer confirmed that there was a fox-sized marmot in the Himalayas that did indeed spread gold dust when digging. At best, what we are left with is an assumption that Herodotus exaggerated in order to fortify a perception of Greek greatness. The fact that he is memorialized around the world in statues and portraits is proof of his success in telling a good story and not bothering with checking the facts of reports he may have heard during his travels. Or as Mark Twain once said, "Never let the truth get in the way of a good story."

Contemporary American culture pays great attention to the exploits of individuals like Miley Cyrus, Britney Spears, or Lyndsay Lohan. We hear a lot about their dishonesty regarding rather trivial concerns that have little impact on the lives of average people. More serious than the untruths told by Miley Cyrus or Britney Spears are presidential lies. More often than not, presidents such as Bill Clinton, Richard Nixon, and Donald Trump make this list. In fact, countless politicians would be on a list of this type along with usual suspects, such as used car salesmen or insurance salesmen. Even Benjamin Franklin is often denounced as a liar because of his claims about his use of a kite and a key in his experiments with lightening, something which modern scientists maintain was not possible.

Perhaps more significant in political terms was his utilization of "fake news" in the newspaper he founded. His best known use of a newspaper to spread lies took place in 1782 while Franklin was in Paris trying to implement a peace treaty between the United States and four European nations. He was also trying to pressure Great Britain into providing reparations to Americans who had been injured by British military actions. His strategy involved the creation of a counterfeit issue of the *Boston Independent Chronicle* newspaper which contained anonymous articles actually written by Franklin himself and intended to support the demand for reparations. By placing copies of this paper with editors of the leading British newspapers, he hoped his articles would be reprinted and be widely read in England. Franklin also ran a false story about the discovery of teenage scalps on the American frontier in an effort to generate hostility toward Native American tribes living in that area. Franklin's experience in using fake stories to undermine his foes enhanced his reputation as a formidable adversary.

Many historians regard the Greeks' wooden Trojan horse as perhaps history's greatest lie. As the Greek-Trojan war entered its tenth year, the Trojans believed that the Greeks were close to the point of surrender. The Greeks presented their giant wooden horse as a peace offering and rolled it into the Trojans' walled city. Not only was the wooden horse a deception, its acceptance by the Greeks was facilitated by the lies of Sinon, an important figure in Greek history. Sinon was said to be an exceptional liar and persuaded the Greeks that the fleeing Trojans were leaving the Trojan horse to honor the victorious soldiers. As the Trojans slept confident of their impending victory, the Greek soldiers who were hidden in the horse came out and killed the Trojan soldiers as well as many civilians. Instead of a victory, the Trojans suffered a great defeat and it was the Greeks who savored the victory. Shakespeare utilized Sinon as a character in several of his plays and presented him as the epitome of treachery and deceit.

Henry VIII was King of England from 1509 until 1547. Early in his reign, Pope Leo X named Henry a Defender of the Faith because of his devout Catholicism. However, he is more remembered for his debauchery, his six marriages, and the execution of wives and political rivals. He was convinced that he was supposed to be head of the church and used every imaginable weapon to make that happen. Because Pope

Clement VII rejected his demand for an annulment of his marriage to Catherine of Aragon, Henry sparked the English Reformation which separated the Church of England from the authority of the Vatican. He had himself named supreme Head of the Church of England and shut down the Catholic convents and monasteries that were the pillars of papal authority. Henry's personal extravagance meant that he was always on the brink of bankruptcy and had to use the funds gained from the sale of the monasteries. He was widely regarded as lustful, egotistical, paranoid and tyrannical. He fabricated criminal charges against political rivals and had many of them executed. The inability of his wife Catherine to provide him with a male heir set Henry on a course that colored the final years of his reign and led to conflicts with Pope Clement VII.

No American figure is more widely reviled for his lies than General Benedict Arnold, whose name is still synonymous with treason. To be described as "a Benedict Arnold" is one of the worst appellations that can be directed against someone. While Arnold enjoyed success in his military service, he always felt that he was underappreciated. He constantly feuded with other generals and demanded more compensation and a higher rank. One year after signing an oath of allegiance, Arnold defected to the British. This action was prompted by promises of money, land, and other benefits for himself and his family. Although the British made him a general, even they regarded him as one of the most notorious liars in history.

Histories of the American West are replete with accounts of legendary figures that are probably more mythical than anything else. One of the best examples is Martha Jane Canary, better known as Calamity Jane. Most information about her early life comes from an autobiographical booklet that was published in 1896. Some historians say this booklet is merely exaggerated, while others claim it is almost completely false. Before her Wild West career began, she was a dishwasher, a cook, a dance hall girl, and even a nurse. As part of her legend, Calamity Jane claimed to have served as an army scout for Wild Bill Hickok and to have fought against the native Americans who attacked settlers. She insisted that she had married Wild Bill and would show a Bible with the date of the wedding and signature of the pastor who performed the service inscribed. Others maintain that this was not true and some asserted that Hickok did not even like Calamity Jane. While there may be little truth in her accounts, they did serve to enshrine her as a heroic Wild West figure.

Calamity Jane, long after her death, has become an Old West legend that embellished her life story to make a modest living. By stark contrast, P. T. Barnum did much to transform entertainment, but is remembered as a deeply dishonest person who accumulated his wealth by exploiting popular gullibility. He came from a family of hucksters and, before he discovered his exceptional skills as an entertainer, he was a newspaper publisher who was convicted of libel. While working in a grocery store, Barnum met an eighty year old slave, Joice Heth, whom he decided to exhibit for entertainment purposes. Because slave ownership was illegal in New York, he arranged to "lease" the elderly lady. To make this exhibit more marketable, he presented her as the 161 year old former nurse of George Washington. To further degrade her appearance, he put her on a diet of only eggs and whiskey. When she was sufficiently drunk, he pulled out all of her teeth in order to make his claim of her advanced age seem plausible. Barnum made an enormous amount of money exhibiting Joice Heth and, when she died in less than a year, he charged admission to look at her autopsy. His next money-making acquisition was a five year old boy who had stopped growing before he was one year old. He called the child "General Tom Thumb."

Using the wealth accumulated in his early years, Barnum opened a five story building in New York City and called it Barnum's American Museum. This operation was a phenomenal success and helped Barnum build a worldwide reputation. The circus for which he is best remembered was essentially his retirement project which he did not start until he was 61 years old. He hosted performances for Abraham Lincoln as well as the queen of England. While known as being perpetually genial and easy going, Barnum was solidly unforgiving of liars. He wrote a long book about this and devoted considerable time exposing spiritualists, con artists, and anyone who would defraud people.

In spite of his history of enriching himself through deception, he insisted that deception was a sin. Barnum, who may have been the ultimate con-man of the 19th century, became a folk hero, and elected to the Connecticut House of Representatives as well as the mayor of Bridgeport.

A more recent case is that of Silvio Berlusconi, an Italian media tycoon and politician who founded a cable television network. Berlusconi was Prime Minister in four governments between 1994 and 2011. He was charged in multiple corruption and bribery trials and in 1998 was given a two year prison sentence on a corruption charge. Although the conviction was overturned, he earned a reputation as being a corrupt serial liar. Even his former friends joined in denouncing him for his lies about his closeness with prostitutes. As a result, the political career of one of Italy's most prominent politicians was destroyed and Italy was plunged into a destructive political crisis. In 2012, Berlusconi was convicted of tax fraud and required to spend one year of community service working at a nursing home. The next year he was convicted of having sex with an underage prostitute as well as abuse of power. He received a seven year sentence that was overturned by an appeals court.

Another person whose name is now synonymous with lying is Charles Ponzi, an almost penniless Italian immigrant who arrived in North America with no means of support. His family in Italy had been reasonably prosperous and sent him to the university. However, he failed to get a degree so his family encouraged him to go to the United States. At one point he worked as a dishwasher in a restaurant and had to sleep on the floor. Eventually, Ponzi created a scheme involving postage stamp speculation and the exchange of international reply coupon (IRC). The IRC could be purchased in Italy and resold in the United States for stamps of a higher value. Investors were promised a 50% return in a mere 90 days. At its peak, this fraudulent investment scheme was bringing great wealth to Ponzi, as much as three million dollars per day in today's money. In 1920, he was charged and convicted of mail fraud and received a five year prison sentence. As a tribute to Ponzi's dishonest character, the term "Ponzi scheme" is a generic term for a corrupt investment arrangement. In 2008, the notorious Bernie Madoff was exposed for following in Ponzi's footsteps with his own investment scam. In what represents one of the biggest lies in history, Madoff's company accumulated more than $50 billion over a ten year period.

Frank Abagnale built a lucrative career out of his skills and his criminal exploits became the subject of a popular film, *Catch Me If You Can*. While still a teenager, Abagnale successfully posed as an airline pilot, an emergency room doctor, and a law school graduate. Eventually, he was exposed and sent to prison because of his fraudulent exploits. After five years, the FBI hired him to work as a specialist helping to investigate fraud cases. As an entrepreneurial person, he founded his own company, Abagnale & Associates, and made a career out of protecting companies from fraud. More recently he published a book entitled *Scam Me If You Can: Simple Strategies to Outsmart Today's Rip-off Artists*, which offers practical advice for individuals to protect themselves against people like he was as a youngster.

The economic scams which can destroy honest fortunes as well as retirement funds for average people are an increasingly common threat in modern societies. In 2020, John McAfee, the former CIO of the anti-virus software company McAfee, was charged with fraud and money laundering. The eccentric 75 year old McAfee, who had been on the run for years, was involved in two cryptocurrency schemes. McAfee had deceived perhaps hundreds of people into investing in his programs. His flamboyant life story was chronicled in the 2016 movie *Gringo*. McAfee committed suicide in his Spanish jail cell in June 2021 just hours after a Spanish court had ruled that he could be extradited to the United States.

While most of these individuals radiate either menace or a destructive greed, Elmyr de Hory was an effective con man whose misdeeds seem relatively benign by comparison. He is widely regarded as the greatest art forger of all time. de Hory began formal training in a Hungarian art colony when he was 16 years old. While he was a gifted artist, he soon realized that his greatest talent was as a forger. After World War II, he moved to the United States where he passed himself off as an impoverished aristocrat who was forced to sell off his valuable art collection. The Hungarian-born de Hory marketed hundreds of forgeries to prominent and prestigious galleries all over the world, and in the process deceived some of the world's most renowned art experts. When his forgeries were finally exposed, buyers were outraged and demanded that he be prosecuted. Since he lived in Spain but had not made any of his sales there, though, he could not be prosecuted. In 1976, de Hory was found dead in his home, apparently as a result of suicide. Given his reputation as a producer of fakes, it is not surprising that many people suspected he had faked his death in order to escape.

It can be especially devastating when a cultural icon is exposed for his dishonesty. In the case of politicians who fall from grace, the impact is less devastating because most politicians are not generally seen as heroes. When President Richard Nixon faced disgrace following exposure of the Watergate break-in, many Americans were disappointed, while others took delight in his misfortune. By contrast, the peccadillos of a philandering Bill Clinton brought joy to some while the more indulgent simply dismissed the amiable southerner as a "rascal."

While it may not affect the fate of the nation, it does undermine popular culture when we lose a figure once seen as inspirational. Athletes fit into this category, as was seen in the cases of the 1919 Chicago "Black" Socks baseball team and of the professional cyclist Lance Armstrong. Unlike politicians, athletes are more often seen as inspirational figures who are admired by the young and the old.

In 1919 the Chicago White Sox had won 88 games and advanced to the World Series to play the Cincinnati Reds. The White Sox first baseman, who had connections with gamblers in Chicago and New York, organized a conspiracy among several teammates to throw the series in exchange for a $100,000 bribe to be paid by a former boxing champion. Fans became suspicious when some of the team's best players performed badly. Their suspicions prompted a grand jury investigation of the dishonest players, who became known as the Black Sox because of their misconduct. The eight players were indicted on conspiracy charges, but when the court's documents were mysteriously lost, the charges were dropped. The only penalty faced by the Black Sox group was to be banned permanently from baseball. An iconic image from the incident was a young boy who during the scandal approached the player "Shoeless" Joe Jackson to implore "say it ain't so Joe."

More recently the cyclist Lance Armstrong was universally admired for his multiple victories in the Tour de France, but also for the fact that he had waged a successful battle against testicular cancer. His image appeared on the covers of sports magazines, as well as on popular general interest periodicals. He was admired by both children and adults, so when there was a controversy over his suspected use of performance-enhancing drugs during his racing wins, everyone wanted to believe it was not true. When Armstrong adamantly and repeatedly denied the accusations people were encouraged and supportive. Eventually, he was forced to admit that the charges were true and he was forbidden to ever race professionally again. This was a personal tragedy for Armstrong but also a disappointment to his millions of fans around the world.

The Emergence of the Con Man

IN 1849, WILLIAM THOMPSON, A CHARISMATIC and charming young man, was arrested by New York City police because he had been approaching complete strangers, befriending them, and convincing them he has an offer that they simply could not refuse. The hapless strangers would then part with much of their money in expectation of some valuable item for a remarkably low price. The item would never appear and William Thompson could not be found. The police described Thompson as a "confidence man." His greatest skill was that he could inspire confidence in gullible people. This was the first time that term had appeared and, as it became more and more common, it was shortened to "con man."

While the charming man who inspired confidence in people was the stereotype for this type of crime, eventually the perpetrators became faceless corporations that inspired confidence by virtue of their size. They could produce slick advertisements about their offerings, so people assumed they must be honest and handed over their money. Whether done by charismatic individuals or by mighty corporations, fortunes were created from the ruined dreams of people whose greatest shortcomings were their trusting natures.

These schemes are more difficult to investigate than traditional lies. The perpetrators are especially cunning and protect themselves with impressive institutions that cloak their real character. They approach their victims with easy smiles and charming banter. Potential victims are met with a sales pitch rather than a threat and they believe they are facing what might be the opportunity of a lifetime. In the end, the victims are delighted to become part of something that may leave them in financial ruin.

One of the greatest clichés about the work of the con man is the suggestion that he could convince you to buy Central Park or the Brooklyn Bridge. Ever since the bridge was completed in 1883, the idea of selling it to an unsuspecting individual was presented as the ultimate expression of the power of persuasion. Con man George Parker was the first person who made a career out of selling the bridge. As immigrants flooded into New York, Parker would often convince the unsuspecting new arrivals that as new Americans one of their best prospects for wealth was to buy the Brooklyn Bridge and charge a fee to every person crossing it. The new "owners" would sign the elaborate documents that Parker created and would then set up a toll booth which policemen would have to remove. Often he was able to make two sales every week and once received $50,000 from a person with more money than sense. He also managed to sell the Metropolitan Museum of Art, the Statue of Liberty and Grant's Tomb. Eventually, Parker was caught, convicted, and sent to Sing Sing prison where he died in 1936. In 1937, a comedy entitled *Every Day's a Holiday* portrayed a con artist named Peaches O'Day—played by Mae West—as she sells the bridge for $200.

In 1901, another individual "sold" the Brooklyn Bridge. He was William McCloundy, who was also known as "I.O.U. O'Brien." For him, this was not much of a career, since he was quickly caught and sent to prison. Even the Eiffel Tower was once "on the market" and actually "sold" twice. When there were news reports that the Eiffel Tower was in need of repairs, a con man named Victor Lustig, who passed himself off as a "Count," forged government documents which identified him as being authorized to sell the Tower for scrap metal. He found two buyers willing to offer him bribes of $200,000 to insure that they would get the contract. Once he had the money, he fled to the United States, where he continued his lucrative career as a swindler.

In the 1890s, a Wild West saloonkeeper and gambling-house owner named Lou Blonger, who was assisted by his brothers, perfected the art of deception with charm rather than guns. He organized a ring of confidence tricksters into what was in effect a union of con men that was based in Denver. Blonger and his brothers operated several saloons and gambling houses. Eventually they added brothels and perfected an illegal lottery known as the "numbers game." At the time, Denver was known as an especially lawless city. Blonger was active in politics and election fraud for both parties. Blonger's ambitions led the gang into more complicated "big cons" that brought in wealthy people. Blonger did not need the relatively small time operations associated with his saloon and moved his headquarters to the American National Bank building. He also found that he did not need the Denver location as his exclusive base and began operations in Miami and Havana. By 1920, Blonger's ambitions exceeded his ability and he approached Republican Party candidate Philip S. Van Cise who was running for district attorney. He offered his electoral fraud services to Van Cise but Van Cise rejected Blonger's offer. Once elected, Van Cise began an investigation aimed at driving Blonger out of business. After a long trial, Blonger and his gang, known as the "Million-Dollar Bunco Ring," were convicted. With his declining health, Blonger entered prison in October 1923 and died in April 1924.

As modernization created new technologies that could be used for illegal purposes, mail fraud became a convenient tool for confidence men. These became scams that far exceeded such cons as the various sales of the Brooklyn Bridge. The biggest mail fraud scheme in history is said to have been the Baker Estate Swindle of 1936. The starting point for this fraudulent operation was that there had been an estate belonging to Colonel Jacob Baker, who had died in 1839 without a will so his huge estate had not been probated and anyone named Baker could possibly gain a share of this huge fortune. Colonel Baker's wealth was based on his ownership of most of the land upon which the city of Philadelphia stood, a tract of land worth $3 billion. For a small fee, anyone named Baker could buy into this legal action and gain a share of the $3 billion. Unfortunately, Colonel Jacob Baker was a fictional creation and there was no estate. William Cameron Morrow Smith, who ran this scam, managed to collect $25 million before he was arrested. Smith's plausible story was based on charm and an intriguing prospect of wealth and did not require force.

Even the world of entertainment was permeated by the machinations of confidence men. In the late 1950s, there were 24 quiz shows which were enormously popular. One of them actually surpassed "I Love Lucy" as the most popular television show of the era. With such intense competition, the shows began to cut corners in an effort to add to the drama and increase their ratings. When the long-time champion of one of the leading shows claimed the show was rigged there was public outrage that sparked Congressional investigations. While nothing could be proven, all of the quiz shows were cancelled. The next entertainment scandal occurred in response to the record industry practice of creating hit songs by giving DJs money to play certain records more often. Known as Payola, the practice was denounced by President Dwight Eisenhower and was branded as a violation of public trust. One instance of this was when Tommy Sands, a teen idol who bore a certain resemblance to Elvis Presley, had a popular single entitled "Teen Age Crush." Its popularity was enhanced when several radio stations played the song continuously for as long as an hour at a time.

In 1988, there was another major mail fraud case involving the largest Christian organization in the world at the time, the Praise the Lord, or PTL, Ministry. Because of a sordid sex scandal, the world—and the government—learned that Jim and Tammy Faye Bakker had been tricking their supporters out of millions of dollars. This was another con based not on force, but on a convincing story line targeting true believers. The targets were willing victims.

During this same period, the Charles Keating Savings and Loan scandal was making headlines as Keating bilked investors out of their life savings. His Lincoln Savings and Loan Company was the vehicle for his activities, which eventually cost taxpayers $3.4 billion. He made reckless stock market investments and contributed millions of dollars to political campaigns. As a tribute to his political influence, five US Senators, led by John McCain, lobbied to prevent charges being filed against Keating for federal civil racketeering and fraud. The "Keating Five" Senators were unsuccessful and Keating was sent to prison.

Other individuals who utilized charm to cheat victims out of millions of dollars were Jordan Belfort and James Paul Lewis Jr. Both were proud of their accomplishments and could not resist the temptation to brag. Belfort's boasts were the most blatant and the book he wrote about his exploits, *The Wolf of Wall Street*, guaranteed him a degree of notoriety that exceeded his actual accomplishment. Made into a movie of the same name, this made him instantly recognizable and ensured that he got an almost two year prison sentence after stealing more than $100 million in his corporate theft scheme.

James Paul Lewis Jr. stole $814 million from thousands of victims in a nationwide scam. His Financial Advisory Consultants firm operated for twenty years but never made any of the investments they promised their investors. This was a typical Ponzi scheme and Lewis relied on trust and word of mouth to convince members of churches and church-related groups to invest their money. He received a thirty year sentence from a judge who described his actions as crimes against humanity.

In 1978, the art of the confidence man reached a new high when the FBI actually recruited a con man to run a con for the federal government. Known as Abscam, the program began with a fairly modest objective which was to find two stolen paintings. The first step involved the creation of Abdul Enterprises, a fake company presumably funded by two Arab sheikhs. The name of the operation—Abscam—is derived from the term "Arab scam." Apparently dizzy with its success, the FBI broadened the Abscam objectives to include a general investigation into governmental corruption. Its method of operation consisted of the phony Arab sheikhs giving officials an opportunity to earn bribes by doing favors for them. Not only were they able to entrap seven members of the US House of Representatives and one US Senator, their operation inspired a highly successful movie entitled *American Hustle*, which received ten Academy Award nominations, thus joining the ranks of films such as *The Wolf of Wall Street* and *Catch Me If You Can*. Apparently, a hallmark of a good scam is that it must have the potential to bring in additional money by becoming an award winning film. The villains can be portrayed as likeable "rascals" who do not leave dead bodies behind when they flee toward their next con. Another unsettling aspect of cons such as these is that they generate questions about the role of federal law enforcement agencies that might undermine the criminal justice process by their active participation in many aspects of the criminal enterprise.

An Abscam innovation was that it featured a scam within a scam. In 1996, the Bayou Hedge Fund Group run by Sam Israel III offered its own innovation when it created the auditing firm that would provide "independent" evaluations of their stock. Because the Bayou Group recommended the technology stocks that were popular at the time, and Israel had a charming demeanor, investors were drawn to the company. But appearances are deceiving, and Bayou was rapidly losing money. Their self-created auditing firm provided salvation in the form of updated financial statements that attracted even more investors whose money could be used to pay off some of the early investors. This was only a short term fix and as Israel's investments continued to fail, the swindler happened to meet another swindler who offered him a way out of his dilemma. This con man convinced Israel that he was a former CIA officer who worked in "black operations" and knew of banks that would support any person who invested in their group. Israel was convinced and invested ten million dollars in what was in reality a high yield investment fraud. For collateral, Israel gave what was supposed to be a pre-World War II Federal Reserve box allegedly containing a $100 million in Federal Reserve "bonds." Not realizing that the Federal Reserve issues notes, not bonds, Israel believed he had escaped from his desperate circumstances. At the time, the FBI was investigating the new con man, rather than Israel, whom they viewed was simply another victim. Realizing that a sophisticated person like Israel should not be involved in such a scheme, the FBI finally recognized that Israel was also a con man. Hoping for a lenient sentence, Israel cooperated with the FBI but still received a 20-year sentence. He made a clumsy effort to fake his suicide, but turned himself in after a three-week flight.

The Enron scandal was a tribute to the dizzying complexity of financial activities in the United States, as well as to the overwhelming greed of the system. The scope of its financial empire was such that it defied conventional investigatory skills. Enron was founded in 1985 and was active in a wide range of markets including energy, commodities, and services. Enron's collapse in 2001 was the largest bankruptcy reorganization in US history at that time; it then had 29,000 employees and enjoyed annual earnings estimated at over $101 billion. For six years in a row, the highly respected Fortune magazine named Enron as the most innovative company in the United States.

While Enron was an American company, in 1991 it began to develop an international component. Because of its recognized stability, Enron was able to reach overseas for energy opportunities and opened a natural gas power plant in the United Kingdom. Its power plant was one of the largest in Europe and produced 3% of the entire electricity requirements of the UK. Because of the success of its ventures in the UK, Enron decided to diversify its global assets under the name Enron International. By 1994, Enron's empire reached The Philippines, Australia, Guatemala, Germany, France, India, China, Japan, and other countries around the world. As if this was not enough, Enron executives set water as their next market expansion. In 1998, it spent almost $3 billion to purchase Britain's Wessex Water Company. This became the core component of a new Enron franchise known as Azurix.

The Azurix venture proved to be the final step in Enron's amazing global expansion. Within two years, Azurix had a modest operating profit and a large debt of $2 billion. British water regulators were demanding a 12% cut in the cost of water plus a costly upgrade of the utility's aging infrastructure. As a result, Enron had no choice but to sell all of the Azurix assets at a tremendous loss. Although Enron hoped to maintain three pipeline companies and most of its international assets, it ended up selling everything. In 2004, the new Enron board of directors took legal action against eleven major institutions which had deceived investors about the true value of Enron. The magnitude of corporate dishonesty became apparent when it was revealed that the Royal Bank of Scotland, Deutsche Bank, and Citigroup were among the defendants.

Theranos and Chernobyl

FEW CONCERNS ARE MORE COMPELLING THAN medical care and public safety. In the United States our need for adequate health care generates intense political debate. In almost every election cycle in the United States, health care rates as one of the most important issues. Given the prominence of this matter, it is not surprising that some of the greatest scams have related to promises of medical breakthroughs that promise to save lives.

In 2014, Elizabeth Holmes, founder and CEO of Theranos, claimed that she had invented a revolutionary machine that would make blood tests faster and easier. Holmes appeared on the cover of *Fortune* and other prestigious business magazines and she was often mentioned as being one of the top business executives in America. Her company enjoyed generous financial support from eager investors and had an estimated value of $9 billion. The Theranos story is one of lying on a massive and destructive scale by utilizing corporate structures for intimidation and public relations stunts. Even Silicon Valley was part of this undertaking. Theranos is widely regarded as perhaps the greatest corporate fraud in US history. Holmes, whose wealth was estimated at $4.5 billion, had a flamboyant manner and was fond of dressing in a style associated with Queen Elizabeth.

Holmes began her preparation of the Theranos marketing plan by meeting with Novartis executives at Novartis in Switzerland. The endorsement by Novartis, as a major drug company in Europe, carried tremendous weight. When their first financial projections did not meet her expectations, Novartis obliged her by adjusting the figures upward in order to attract investors. Eventually, Rupert Murdoch became the main Theranos investor. In building Theranos, Holmes decried the fact that each year a hundred thousand American died from adverse drug reactions and claimed her blood monitoring technology would prevent that tragedy. She turned to Silicon Valley to enlist people to help her tailor drugs to individuals. Some of the most successful people in the tech world—such as several who helped create the iPhone— eagerly joined her crusade.

While she talked about the good that would be done by Theranos, her greatest energy was devoted to making it a quick commercial success. One of her most important initiatives was lobbying for passage of a bill in Arizona that would allow patients to get a blood test without doctors' orders. In 2015, the bill was passed and opened up an important avenue for Theranos. Holmes' grandiose claims about Theranos technology were never backed up by peer-reviewed data. She relied more on an emotional pitch about a technology that would prevent people from having to say goodbye to loved ones whose premature deaths could have been prevented by Theranos.

Holmes resisted anyone who suggested she should slow down and wait for the technology to work. When _The Wall Street Journal_ ran a series of critical articles, Holmes responded with threats of legal action. With her abundant resources, she was able to overwhelm her adversaries in long and expensive court proceedings. Many of the people on her staff were noted for their aggressive, menacing styles and there were bitter confrontations with those she saw as rivals.

Even though Theranos was a medical product, the main people responsible for its development were mechanical engineers and public relations specialists. The company's marketing campaign focused on creating a brand identity and a Smartphone app that would link to Theranos services. They targeted the Safeway grocery store chain—a company that needed a boost in order to stabilize its financial position— and Walgreens pharmacy as vehicles for Theranos. The goal was to place Theranos devices in each of their many stores. The first Theranos "wellness center" was set up in a Walgreens store in Palo Alto, California.

The "engine" for the Theranos technology was a _nanotainer_. It was is a tiny vial, less than half an inch tall, that would hold a few drops of blood for testing. The *nanotainer* worked like a plunger that would create a vacuum that would push the blood into the vial. In the first tests, the *nanotainer* exploded and splattered blood everywhere. Homes seemed indifferent to such setbacks and pushed for tests that were carefully calculated to produce the desired results.

In 2015, skeptics were raising questions about the efficacy of Theranos's technology. By 2017, the company's value—which was once in the billions—had plummeted to zero. It officially closed in 2018, fifteen years after its founding. Theranos' collapse was a result of examinations of its work by the overseer of clinical laboratories in the United States. In Arizona and California a million Theranos test results were found to be flawed. Two employees of the company became disillusioned and reported their suspicions to authorities. Holmes was charged with nine counts of wire fraud and two counts of conspiracy to commit wire fraud. These charges were based on allegations that she engaged in a scheme to defraud investors and an effort to defraud doctors and patients. Even though she faced the prospect of 20 years in prison, Holmes continued to live in luxury as she pushed for delays in her trial date. In a court filing in March 2021, both defense attorneys and prosecutors asked the judge for a six week delay of the start of her trial because of her pregnancy.

As her trial date approached, attorneys for Holmes advanced a novel defense strategy. Using the services of a forensic psychologist and Cal State Fullerton professor, they advanced the argument that Holmes suffered from a mental condition that undermined her judgment. They maintained that as a result she could not form the intent to actually lie. Therefore, since lying requires intent to deceive, Holmes could not be found guilty.

The Theranos case is especially troubling because the perfidy, greed, and reckless indifference to the health of customers were associated with so much of the American elites. Those people who benefited from the privilege of the American system should have been among those who ensured that the system was operating properly. A further problem of this case is that it defies the normal manner in which lies should be detected. The skills that otherwise would have offered some protection against such people were less applicable because of the magnitude of the scandal.

In the United States there are few incidents with greater potential for damage to public health than the Theranos scandal. However, in the Soviet Union, the most devastating example of the consequences of official dishonesty is the 1986 Chernobyl nuclear meltdown incident. And, still worse, in the case of Chernobyl, the full consequences of the nuclear disaster have been felt for years. With Theranos, we can at least take comfort in knowing that medical consequences were avoided.

After the Chernobyl disaster on April 26, 1986, thousands of Soviet citizens were diagnosed with cancer and suffered horrible deaths. Most people remember that this tragedy was a result of a failed nuclear reactor safety test. Fewer people are aware of the network of lies and evasions associated with the explosion of the reactor. In the first days after the meltdown, Soviet authorities remained silent and on May Day the huge parade in nearby Kiev proceeded as if there was no problem. It was not until monitoring stations in Europe noticed elevated radiation levels that there was a discussion about what might have happened.

Even after admitting that there had been an explosion, Soviet scientists would not acknowledge how high the radiation levels had become. Nor was there an open discussion about the need for a wider containment zone. Although the new Soviet leader Mikhail Gorbachev promised openness and transparency, the Kremlin was more concerned about maintaining its image of strength as a global superpower. Within the Soviet scientific community there had long been a realization of the weaknesses of Chernobyl's design. This information, if discussed, could have led to changes that would have prevented the failure of the safety test that led to the explosion. Scientists were instructed to hide the flaws and not to discuss those flaws even among themselves.

After the explosion, thousands of Soviets—both civilians and military—volunteered to work on the cleanup of the reactor. Within a few years, efforts ceased because all of those volunteers had died. The story of Chernobyl helps us see the consequences in terms of lives lost due to terminal cancer. However, as could be seen with Theranos, the lies were on such an exalted scale and the liars were protected by those in power, that it is almost impossible to engage in the sort of interrogation or investigation that might reveal the truth.

The Costs of Undetected Deceit

WHEN LOOKING AT THE LIES OF popular cultural icons like Brittany Spears, the consequences of their deceptions are minimal and perhaps even amusing since few people have true reverence for popular entertainers. By contrast the lies of Pope Alexander VI cultivated the corruption of that era and greatly enriched him and his family. As a result of these personal gains, it is possible to give him credit for the work he performed in advancing art and his promotion of negotiation as an alternative to war.

Of course, the notorious Trojan horse episode demonstrated the powerful impact of lies and deception. Coupled with the Trojans' overconfidence, this maneuver completely reversed the course of the decade-long war between Troy and the Greeks. The Trojans were doomed by their hubris and inability to discern the truth of the event unfolding before them.

Benjamin Franklin's dishonesty, especially his utilization of "fake news" through his counterfeit newspapers, contributed to the overall climate of politics during the era of the Revolutionary War. His lies, while interesting and effective in undermining his adversaries, stimulated a popular cynicism that continued long after Franklin's disappearance from American politics.

The lies and deceptions of Henry the VIII plunged England into political turmoil that lasted well beyond his death. Scottish unrest continued to become an almost permanent feature of political life and Oliver Cromwell's disruptive role exacerbated this situation. Eventually Cromwell was charged with treason and executed.

Benedict Arnold's lies constituted a threat to the survival of the

American Revolution. His betrayal of his comrades was shameful and the military secrets he divulged resulted in the deaths of many soldiers in the Revolutionary Army. His betrayal was not motivated by any particular values but simply by his greed and pride. It is significant that when he went to Britain, he was not held in high regard by the people whose cause he advanced.

The cost of the deceptions of P. T. Barnum had no impact on history or politics. One can even suggest that people such as General Tom Thumb had no real talents and that Barnum did them a favor because his exploitation of such people gave them the ability to make money. Upon his death, Tom Thumb was wealthy and had a family. On the other hand, he took money from millions of people who trusted and respected him.

Undoubtedly one of the most disastrous examples of the cost of undetected lies was the Chernobyl disaster. It is impossible to make an accurate assessment of the damage that flowed from this horrible incident. The short-term loss of life was devastating, but the long-term impact on the health of more thousands has yet to be seen. The property loss can already be seen as thousands of people lost their homes and all of their possessions.

Most of these examples demonstrate the ability of criminals to enrich themselves at the expense of a gullible public. They show how cynical politicians have been able to manipulate circumstances in such a way as to undermine the stability of their communities. These grandiose figures usually operate on an elevated public platform and are harder to expose and defeat.

It is the less exalted villains who pose a more direct threat. These are the often petty criminals whose actions lead to the deaths of innocent people or the espionage agents who elude counter intelligence officers and pass national security information to our adversaries. This is the arena—focused on specific incidents rather than on a lifetime of corruption—in which the detection and exposure of falsehoods and deceptions is immediately relevant.

Even more relevant to the consideration of the costs of undetected lies are the advertisements for cigarettes. In the 1940s, the lung cancer death rate was steadily increasing but medical research had not focused on cigarette as the cause. In 1930, the American Tobacco company created an ad that claimed "20,679 Physicians say 'LUCKIES are less irritating'" to the throat. The American Tobacco company's ad agency had sent cartons of Lucky Strike cigarettes to thousands of doctors along with a letter asking them if they thought these cigarettes would irritate users' throats less than other cigarettes. Not surprisingly, thousands responded and agreed with the statement. While a throat irritation was less significant than cancer, the suggestion was that Lucky Strikes were in some way medically superior.

In 1937, the Philip Morris Company organized a project in which doctors compared Phillip Morris cigarettes to others and concluded that when people switched to Phillip Morris, every case of throat irritation cleared up. These findings were used to create an advertisement that appeared in one of the most popular magazines in the United States. This theme appeared in their advertisements throughout the 1940s.

Using the same technique, in 1946 R.J. Reynolds Tobacco Company created a Medical Relations Division. Through this organization, R. J. Reynolds paid for research that was calculated to put their products in a favorable light. Company representatives would attend medical conventions and pass out cartons of their cigarettes to anyone who would take them. This eventually allowed them to create the slogan "more doctors smoke Camels than any other cigarette." They were able to employ this slogan for years in their advertising campaigns.

During this time, more and more cigarette companies created advertisements featuring images of idealized physicians who looked wise and caring. The pictures were never of real doctors who could be identified, since doctors were not allowed to advertise. The ad companies selected actors who fit the desired image. To add variety to their pictures, the companies would focus on figures such as cowboys, businessmen wearing fashionable suits, and any figure with whom an average man working in an office or a factory could identify. Cigarette advertisements stressed images and brand loyalty. The cigarette you smoked was intended to create an identity for you. A popular song of the period contained the lyrics "he can't be a man because he doesn't smoke the same cigarette as me!" In 1962, the Marlboro Man, who was a handsome cowboy, appeared and this marked the image of Marlboro cigarettes for decades. All of this was a reflection of life-style and sophistication. Smokers were portrayed as people who were prosperous and were having fun. When women began to smoke, the advertisements showed this as a feature of a modern environment with the women being young, attractive, and wearing the newest fashions.

The damage wrought by cigarette smoking has been overwhelming, and cancer caused by smoking has become one of our main killers. But the question within the context of exposing lies is a difficult one. It is not simply a matter of statistics that can be checked in some way. It was only in later years, for example, that we learned that the Marlboro Man featured in the ads had died of lung cancer. The challenge in dealing with this type of lie is to identify the specific untruth. How do you challenge an ad that implies you will be socially accepted and happy if you use a certain product?

We like to think of lies, or even deceptions, as being based or not based on verifiable facts. But an ad campaign uses images, something that is difficult to explicitly refute. Moreover, an ad campaign encompasses several themes and more than one apparent factual statement. This falls within the world of psychological operations and is best countered by an opposing campaign. Building a defense against a psychological operations campaign is complicated and requires specific countervailing arguments. Obviously, smoking is still common but it is down in terms of usage. The factors contributing to its decline can be found in legal restrictions on marketing of cigarettes. The television advertisements that were once seen everywhere have been eliminated. Even the health warnings on cigarette packages represent counter propaganda. Finally, there is an abundance of information about the health risks of smoking. In 2018, 14% of American adults smoked while in 1965 42% of Americans were smokers. Statistics clearly show that smoking is continuing to decline and will likely continue to decline as the national health care debate continues.

Classifications of Lies

I F WE HOPE TO DETECT LIES, it is important to begin with an examination of the classifications of lies and the factors which motivate people to lie. The psychologist Leo Buscaglia, political philosopher Hannah Arendt, polygraph expert Leonard Saxe, and the German philosopher Friedrich Nietzsche are but a few of those who have studied and categorized types of lies. Psychologists and neuroscientists, in their studies of serial killers, have speculated that such individuals exhibit a chromosomal abnormality that causes them to have a sense of detachment from society. As a result, they feel no guilt about lying. Long ago Nietzche maintained that lying was simply a condition of life.

In a more general sense, sociologists and psychologists conclude that our widespread acceptance of lying has resulted in an erosion of cultural values. Even petty, mundane lies contribute to this environment. A person who can justify his lie as a way to avoid making someone feel bad can more easily reconcile telling a more serious lie in order to advance his personal interests. A painfully obvious point is that while not all lies are the same, they are all exercises in deception.

In *Loving Each Other: The Challenge of Human Relationships*, psychologist Leo Buscaglia identifies several specific types of lies. As you consider each of these, you will recognize that there will be different tactics required to detect each of them. Most people will at some time use the benevolent lie as part of an effort to avoid offending someone. Instead of saying that your friend's parties are all dull, you can suggest that you have a previous commitment that night. Other lies are self-protective and used to help you avoid getting in trouble. Rather than get into an argument over an apparent insult, you can simply say that you were misunderstood or your statement was out of context. Other lies are manipulative and designed to help you get your way. If a person is campaigning for a promotion in his office, he might make contradictory promises to people who do not interact with each other in an effort to secure their support. Finally, there is the status lie that people often use as a way of pretending that they are more important or prosperous than they really are. As a joke, we often see a person driving an old, unattractive car with a bumper sticker which proclaims his other car is a Mercedes. In addition to these types of lies there are lies that advance a cover-up or a conspiracy. The Watergate scandal required a number of cover-up lies and Aron Burr used lies to advance the conspiracy that insured his notorious place in history.

Success in this regard begins with an understanding of why people tell lies. There are times when a suspect will indicate that he simply has no reason to lie. By examining motives, you can better determine if the suspect has any reason to lie. Random studies, both scientific and non-scientific, show that the average person lies at least ten times each day, while some people may lie at least two hundred times each day. In your personal relationships, this understanding helps you navigate the intrigue of a community. If you can do this, it may be helpful in a personal way but your life and national security are not dependent upon this talent.

Depending on the method of analysis, there are several explanations for why people lie. If you want to understand how to assess the honesty of people with whom you interact, you need to identify the most common reasons that motivate people to lie. In our casual social lives, we recognize that—with the best of intentions—people tell white or benevolent lies as Leo Buscaglia noted in his classification of lies. People who tell white lies justify that by saying they did not want to make someone feel bad. If you receive a gift that you loathe, you may well gush over the gift saying it is what you have always wanted. Assuming you do not make the mistake of "re-gifting" the unwanted item, you may have avoided a social affront that would have resulted from your absolute honesty. From the viewpoint of the analyst that needs to determine the reliability of this person, a propensity to tell white lies does not impeach the integrity of the teller, but it is important to make note of this relatively minor example of dishonesty.

Closely related to this type of polite lie but not mentioned in the Leo Buscaglia classification is the failure to honor a commitment. A person may promise to do something to help a friend, but as the time of performance nears, he realizes he cannot do that and simply does not appear. This is more significant than the white lie and may jeopardize an important program. The person who does this is more suspect and less reliable that the teller of white lies. Your assessment of the reliability of this person will necessarily be relatively low and you should be skeptical about depending on him.

A fabrication is a different and more dangerous form of lying. It refers to the relaying of information that a person simply does not know is false. Generally, this is motivated by a desire to injure someone and falls into the world of deception and psychological operations. Recognizing this fabrication is difficult and your success may rest on knowing the reputation of the person who is telling the story. Here you must consider the record of the informant who gives you this information.

The bold-faced lie is based on repetition of something which is generally known to be untrue but the informant is hoping to create confusion or to undermine the reputation of his target. Hearing such an untruth will make an intelligent person feel resentment against anyone who would waste their time with having to hear an account that may be regarded as an "insult to their intelligence." Nonetheless, the bold-faced lie can serve the purpose of wasting the time of an investigator.

An exaggeration is a blend of truth and lies. Part of the story is true but the informant feels a need to embellish the truth. He has told part of the truth but has added to it to make his testimony seem more valuable and his importance to the investigator even greater. The difficulty of detecting an exaggeration is the element of truth that serves as the foundation for this untruth. Many interrogators want to accept whatever truth they find and see it as evidence of overall truthfulness.

If you have a source prone to exaggeration, you will have to discount the value of his information.

Deception is a form of lie that endeavors to create a false impression. Deception is a basic part of a psychological operations campaign since it helps build a misleading impression. In military operations it has been the decisive factor between achieving victory or being handed a defeat. Deception provides the element of surprise in combat operations and, in this respect, is a deadly form of lie. The person who practices deception does not proclaim the truth of his lies, but waits for his enemy to reach an inaccurate conclusion and act upon the basis of that conclusion. As the allies planned for the D-Day invasion in June 1944, deception was a major part of their planning and is regarded as instrumental in the success of the invasion.

While of less strategic importance, plagiarism is another form of lying. If you realize that your informant has submitted a report which was based largely on the research of another person, you cannot accept the credibility of that person. Politicians have occasionally stolen speeches from successful leaders in an effort to replicate their success. The people who need to be able to detect practitioners of plagiarism are usually journalists, although teachers are also alert to this.

When conducting an investigation, it is vital to know if you have an informant who is a compulsive liar. Police officers are likely to encounter such people who seem ready to confess to a variety of crimes, not because they are guilty of committing those crimes but simply because they crave attention. If the investigator has access to good records, he will usually identify such a person. In many countries a person's confession cannot be accepted until he provides corroboration of his actions on the basis of information not released to the press.

Sam Vaknin, who is the author of the book *Malignant Self Love*, runs the website Malignant Self Love—Narcissism Revisited. He offers his own classification system for an examination of the phenomenon of lying. His classification system includes eight types of lies. The first type is referred to as utilitarian because it is designed to accomplish a specific goal. A first step in divining such a lie is to identify the broader type of activity in which the subject is involved.

The second type, the smokescreen, appears most often in espionage or military operations and its purpose is to obscure true information as a way of deceiving others. The third is the compassionate lie or, as Buscaglia called it, the white lie. This type of lie recognizes the sensitivities or vulnerabilities of other people and is an effort to spare their feelings. Most social orders require rankings in order to determine who is on top and who is on the bottom. The fourth type of lie is ceremonial and is reflected in manners or good etiquette. The way in which we address a person who holds a senior position—Sir or Your Honor—will be a reflection of their status within the community. The fifth type of lie is compensatory and is a fiction intended to hide the fact that you do not actually know the truth. Creating a fiction is preferable to muttering that you have no idea. The next type of lie is the confabulation. It is a lie intended to boost or protect one's self-esteem. The confabulator realizes he is lying but his lie has an element of truth. Perhaps he was actually in the marathon race although he did not come in first, for example. The confabulation can be regarded as an entertaining deviation of the truth that is designed to protect the grandiose feelings of a narcissist. Most people will stumble into logical fallacies without intending to lie. What this amounts to is an inferential lie, which is Vaknin's seventh category. This takes us back to Jimmy Carter's declaration "I will never knowingly lie to you."

The final category is the hybrid lie. As the name suggests, this lie contains both false and true elements. It is often associated with dictatorships in which the government makes statements that reflect truth but only if you understand the realities of your environment. When the East German government constructed the Berlin Wall and its other border fortifications, it was referred to as the anti-fascist protective barrier. Citizens were told these barriers were designed to protect them from Westerners trying to illegally enter East Germany. Most of the population understood that the wall was built to keep the East Germans from leaving. Reports about the wall revealed the truth to knowledgeable citizens who realized that the wall was erected because more and more people had been leaving. The government did not have to proclaim the truth, but most people knew the wall was designed to keep East Germans inside the country.

The classifications of lies serve in analyzing lies in a general sense. However, these classifications should not obscure the complexity of telling lies. While you might identify a specific untrue statement and insert it within one of these categories, you have not demonstrated an ability to find the truth hidden by the lies. In practice, most of these classifications are blended into a "recipe" that is intended to accomplish an objective. In military history, a study of Operation Mincemeat reveals a combination of lies or suggestions intended to influence the military decisions of the German forces in World War II. It was a subtle concoction intended as misdirection and to convince the Germans that the Allied attack would be on Greece or Sardinia. You could not place that operation within one classification because it is better understood by the intentions of the Mincemeat planners.

Types of Liars

WHILE IT IS IMPORTANT TO LOOK at types of lies, it is equally important to consider the types of liars and to understand the various levels of the types of liars. In many, but not all ways, this typology corresponds to the characterization of lies noted above. It is important to recognize that lying does not always involve telling you something that is not true. However, the details that they omit from their accounts transform the otherwise truthful statement into a deception.

The first type is referred to as the white liar, a person who sees his lies as beneficial in that they make someone feel better. His lies are often a function of his social environment. Within his family, he would be reluctant to tell his wife that her new dress is unflattering. Since this type of liar usually is at least telling some of the truth, it is possible he does not feel he is actually lying. After all, he sees this as something fairly insignificant.

Another type of liar is the careless liar, who tends to lie all of the time. He has no concern about the ethical aspects of his lies but is motivated by an inability to formulate a truthful account of something being discussed. It is simply easier for him to tell a lie and he likely does not even give it a thought.

The occasional liar is a person who does not habitually lie. He is likely to feel guilty about having lied as it is something he might have done to avoid embarrassment had he acknowledged a shortcoming. If confronted in a professional or personal setting, the occasional liar will usually ask for forgiveness.

Compulsive liars are people whose dishonesty is habitual. They

tell lies when they don't have to or even when the truth would better serve their interest. If someone is a product of an environment
in which no disagreement or disappointment was acceptable, he may
have developed lying as his default response to routine questions. He
would determine what answer was acceptable and offer that response.
The compulsive liar is not manipulative or malicious. He lies because
it is a habit and less demanding than developing a candid, truthful
response. Because he has a lot of practice, the compulsive liar may be
very smooth and engaging. He is entertaining and plausible because
he believes his own lies. Of course, such a person is not trustworthy
and is forced to devote a lot of his time coming up with new, interesting stories to embellish his personal narrative.

The most destructive type of liar is the sociopathic liar, who is incapable of feeling shame, remorse, or guilt. Lying is simply his life strategy and he uses this in an effort to get whatever he wants. He could
seek a promotion in the work place or to gain the upper hand in a personal relationship. Sociopathic liars are often charismatic and charming individuals, and many of them rise to the top of their professional
fields, largely because they have no problem getting ahead by stepping
on the backs of those with whom they work. When confronting such
a person, it is essential to have all of the evidence you need to prove
he has lied. If your goal is to discern the truth, you must be confident
of your evidence. You also need to recognize that the sociopathic liar
is unlikely to admit to his lies or to change his behavior.

Who Lies More?

G ENDER ISSUES HAVE ASSUMED GREAT IMPORTANCE in recent years. While we think about gender divisions in terms of issues such as equal pay for men and women, it is interesting to look at the question of which gender is more likely to lie.

If you look at discussions of this interesting question simply as entertainment and likely seen on a television program, there is a consensus that men lie more often than women. In 2017, the British tabloid *Express* endeavored to conduct a survey that might lend a fraction of academic legitimacy to this debate. Their survey results indicated that men were more likely to lie, as 10% admitted to regular lying and a third of that group acknowledged the lies were serious. Over 25% of all respondents, both male and female, admitted they did not fully trust their partners. Other surveys indicate that men are more prone to infidelity than women.

In contrast to the survey done by the British newspaper in 2017, when greater methodological rigidity is imposed, academic surveys indicate that men and women lie at an equal rate. This changes if one takes into account the issue of when men lie to women as compared to when men lie to men. There is equal complexity when surveys studied women lying to men as opposed to women lying to other women. Results also varied in terms of the types of lies being examined. Finally, studies indicate that as people age, they lie less. That may be a function of opportunity and the size of the community within which an elderly person functions. If you are not around many people, you have fewer opportunities to lie.

Given the disparity of results in supposedly "scientific" studies, this is a question that cannot be definitively answered. While gender may be a factor in dishonesty, there are other more important factors that impinge on this behavior. Most men will always be convinced their ex-wives lie and most women will have the same view of ex-husbands.

A more important direction when considering who lies more is to look at certain professions. In a negative category, it is hard to beat politicians and television news, but many other professions are also viewed with distrust. By contrast, doctors, nurses, and pharmacists are our most highly respected professions. The military and the police, in spite of recent complaints, are highly regarded by most citizens. Small businesses, contrasted with large corporations, are highly regarded for the role they play in our communities. Generally, regardless of how the survey is conducted, politicians are viewed as the least trustworthy of professions. This is ironic when you consider that people distrust the politicians whom they put in office. More important is the fact that we don't trust those who make decisions for us; this clearly undermines faith in the institutions that govern our society.

There are numerous surveys intending to identify the professions that are most or least trusted. After politicians, newspaper journalists are among the least trusted professions and the most likely to indulge in lying. Real estate agents, insurance sales people, and mechanics are distrusted by most people, although there is a greater degree of trust in our own mechanics. After all, your car is still running, so he deserves some credit for that happy result. On the other hand, most people have had a bad experience involving a lawyer and this profession is widely distrusted. The fact that doctors, our most trusted professionals, feel threatened by malpractice attorneys does not endear them to most people.

The 2021 Edelman Trust Barometer documented the erosion of trust in institutions. This includes not only government but also business, the media, and non-governmental organizations. The survey indicated that at least 57% of the population believes the United States is on the verge of civil war. This is coupled with a growing distrust of the elites as a class of people responsible for the management and leadership of important institutions.

The idea that political and professional elites are trustworthy has been essential to the survival of our pluralist, representative democracy for two-and-a-half centuries. The idea of a free state in which decisions were made by the entire community—the iconic New England small town—was eroded by population growth. With that came a practical realization that a smaller group of people should be selected to represent community interests and deliberate over policy. These "elders" were people who were trusted. As the system became more complex, there was a greater need for professional expertise but the average citizen who had time and motivation knew he could research the process because he had access to the reports, accounts, records and testimonies used by the elites. He trusted that these documents were accurate and that events were being faithfully and fully reported.

This system was based on trust that the elites worked on behalf of the community interest rather than on their own self-interest. The system was maintained even when it became apparent that the entire elite network—government, media, the corporate work, law, and academia—were working in unison on the basis of their shared interests and values. When little by little the public learned about scandals and corruption, this system was weakened. Critics identified two types of knowledge that shaped policy. The first was the special access network based on insider ties while the other type was common knowledge that rejected the insiders' claims of professional expertise. In politics there were endless revelations about how contracts were given for publicly funded projects. In economics the erosion was accelerated by things such as insider trading that involved business elites. These revelations fueled a growing distrust in elites and the institutions they dominated. The faith required to sustain trust was steadily undermined.

As a result, the honesty of most senior officials and politicians is no longer automatically accepted. Especially during the long age of Covid restrictions when those people were making decisions that had costly, if not deadly, impacts on the average citizen, there was a growing distrust of the elites who were benefiting from the political administrative system. This fueled the views of citizens attracted by the populist critiques of elites seen as isolated from real world struggles. The argument that self-serving elites worked to maintain a system that empowered and protected them was no longer a theme advanced only by conspiracy theorists. Of course, smug elites may assure each other that everybody knows such accusations are false but the sad truth is that tens of millions of average citizens of the non-elite variety embrace those assertions.

In April of 2021, the technical director of CNN was recorded boasting to his date about how his network collaborated to determine the outcome of the 2020 election. Although having himself recorded exposing how CNN worked to mislead their viewers probably came as a shock to his bosses, it merely affirmed the beliefs of people already disposed to see the network as part of the elites who looked down on the unsophisticated residents of "flyover" country.

The "Science" of Body Language

A S IS OFTEN NOTED, NOT ALL communication is verbal. Verbal communication is easier to understand because the words tell us what the subject intends to say. Of course, the spoken words may be designed to mislead the listeners. The subject can speak in a way intended to mislead; he can learn to speak in another language. But his body language may reveal things hidden by his words. Body language, especially intentional body language, may reinforce points made by the speaker. An arm wave or a fist banging on the table can be part of the process of communication. For years scholars studied the speaking style of Adolph Hitler. His gestures were intentional and he apparently practiced them in front of a mirror as he prepared for a speech. This was all part of his intentional body language. Similarly, in the 1940s and 1950s, teams of "Sovietologists" at the CIA spent countless hours examining video and still photographs of those officials in proximity to Soviet leader Stalin, hoping to discern some intelligence insights based on his body language toward them.

As we begin an effort to create a science of body language, the starting point must be the identification of what constitutes the baseline of behavior. This means determining normal behavior for an individual or for a group. By recognizing an anomaly from baseline behavior, it is possible to see how a person has reacted to the interviewer's question. If the interviewer's question is shocking or surprising to the subject, it is likely that his behavior will deviate from the baseline norm. Sometimes there are technological innovations that can measure this deviation. A good example of this technology is the polygraph which measures reactions but does not always reveal what those reactions mean.

The study of body language as an interrogation technique is associated with the Reid technique, an approach widely used by police in North America which has nine steps in the interrogation process. There is a widespread assumption that the system does not take into account cultural factors that drive specific body language. Critics maintain that this technique is fundamentally flawed and has produced confessions from innocent people.

Even more difficult to understand than conventional body language is unintentional body language. This includes motions or even gestures a person makes without intending to do so. When confronted with especially damaging information during interrogation, the suspect's face may turn red. Most people cannot control this reaction so the interrogator must make a judgment about why the person's face has turned red. Is it guilt, embarrassment, or shock? Embarrassment is a self-conscious emotion that has a negative impact on the thoughts or behavior of the target. A propensity for embarrassment is affected by cultural factors. Culture will shape human behavior, interaction, and thought patterns. Therefore, what embarrasses an American might have no impact on a German or an African. Having some understanding of the culture of the person being interrogated will help to understand their self-conscious reactions.

Body language is affected by a variety of factors, including cultural traits. Diverse cultural environments will make an examination of body language more challenging. The cultural foundations of body language will drive a person's understanding of the reactions of the subject of his interrogations. Americans typically feel that a person who makes eye contact is more trustworthy because within the context of Western culture making eye contact is seen as a positive expression of body language. In Eastern culture, making eye contact is seen as somewhat aggressive and should not be a prolonged action. In many Asian societies it is seen as respectful or deferential to look away from a person who is in a position superior to your own. In Western culture nodding is seen as a gesture of agreement while in Central Asia it indicates disagreement. An American who is hitching a ride will face traffic with his thumb extended in hopes of getting that ride. A US soldier who has just arrived in Saudi Arabia and is attempting to hitch a ride as he would in the United States probably would not realize that the thumb out gesture was offensive in that country, and would earn him a beating.

Something as basic as a smile can have vastly different meanings depending on the circumstances under which the person smiles. If the smile is honest or sincere, the eyes will crinkle and the lips will turn up at the corners. This is what people mean when they refer to whether or not someone's smile reaches the eyes. If it does not, there is an assumption that the smile is not sincere. If the interviewer sees the smile as a smirk or partial smile, his analysis should regard this as a *micro expression* of contempt, rather than a positive indication. It could signal a negative reaction and mean the subject's response is not honest. However, if in a social setting the subject holds eye contact with the interviewer for a longer period of time, this should be accepted as an indication of sincerity, honesty, or even attraction to the interviewer. All of these factors will be obscured during times such as the Covid-19 pandemic with its requirements for the wearing of facemasks.

Studies often undermine traditional popular conceptions about body language. Many people believe that rapid blinking is an indication of deception. However, while rapid blinking is associated with stress, the blinking does not necessarily indicate deception. More often it simply means the person is worried about something, is uncomfortable, or is considering an issue related to the interview. None of that constitutes proof of deception. A person's lips also tell a story that does not always mean he is lying. Narrowed lips can indicate disagreement or being uncomfortable. Slightly parted lips, however, indicate that a person is relaxed or comfortable. All of these reactions can mean something, but dishonesty is not necessarily the only meaning.

Culture even affects how people react to various forms of discomfort, including severe physical pain. People from the southern Mediterranean and the Middle East are expected to express pain and suffering. The emotional displays during funerals in those regions are an expression of this tendency. In other cultures, such emotion is discouraged and viewed as a weakness. The English were once known for their expression of the need to "keep a stiff upper lip." In 1808, the English author Fanny Burney offered to hold her cancerous breast while doctors removed it without anesthetics of any sort. Burney's reaction was shaped by an English culture that expected people to be brave in the face of severe agony. During combat, English soldiers would endure the pain associated with the removal of limbs under primitive medical circumstances. In a similar fashion, Confucian cultures required people to keep their pain to themselves and never share it with others.

In the 21st century, advances in medicine have made it possible for people to avoid pain. In the Soviet Union, people who went to the dentist knew there were no painkillers and would comfort themselves with tremendous amounts of vodka in advance, and afterward they accepted the inevitable misery of the recovery period. Western medical advances enabled people to reject the idea that pain was heaven-sent and an inevitable part of the human condition. Those who once believed that a lifetime of pain would be assuaged in the afterlife now expect doctors to provide an infinite variety of pain medications. It is not surprising that the most common addiction of the 21st century is to opioids, the most powerful pain medicine of this time.

A crucial factor in assessing truthfulness is the recognition of social boundaries which are determined by our cultural requirements. Working with a person from Turkey, for example, you will learn that their idea of social distance is measured in inches. A meaningful conversation will be conducted in an almost face to face manner in which you will be aware of what the Turk had for dinner. In stark contrast, an American or an Englishman will want to be at a much greater distance. Training for Foreign Area Officers in the US Army devotes considerable attention to recognizing social boundaries without needlessly offending those with whom you work in a military or social environment.

Body language can also be affected by certain mental conditions. This is particularly true of severe social anxiety which may create difficulties for someone to directly face another person. It is likely to make a person reluctant to have any physical contact, including shaking hands. A person who suffers from social anxiety will exhibit symptoms that, if not properly diagnosed, will make the subject seem very suspicious or guilty. This would be a misleading assumption.

A person with social anxiety will seem very nervous, worried, or simply incapable of dealing with ordinary affairs. Severe anxiety will make the sufferer appear incapable of functioning and make his statements seem unreliable or untrue. Because this condition can last for years, the sufferer will start to view his condition as perfectly normal (if only for him) and will not seek treatment or be able to explain his difficulties. It is estimated that as many as 15% of American adults suffer from social anxiety.

There are consistent observable symptoms that social anxiety sufferers exhibit. One of the most obvious is panic attacks, which will occur when there is no apparent threat and will result in rapid heartbeat, sweating, shaking, or an inability to speak. In a similar fashion, the person with social anxiety will appear to be under great stress even in what would be regarded as restful times. He will engage in repetitive behavior and will embrace certain rituals, such as checking again and again to determine if a door is actually closed. Upon leaving his home, he will be forced to return to check on routine things, such as whether the lights are turned off. He is also likely to display excessive self-consciousness, making it impossible for him to be around groups of people.

There are debilitating physical conditions associated with such anxiety. There can be an irregular heartbeat as well as sweating or trembling. It may bring about hyperventilation and make concentration very difficult, if not impossible. This is also associated with sleep deprivation and a feeling of impending doom. A person in this condition may be unable to complete routine tasks associated with his job and will be unable to provide accurate information about his surroundings or situation. An effort to determine this person's honesty is likely to be a futile undertaking because the individual is unable to make coherent observations.

If your goal is a degree of communication that will help you make judgments about the honesty of a person, it is vital to take into account the full range of both verbal and non-verbal communications. This includes active or empathic listening, a process in which the listener repeats what the person whom he is questioning has said.

Forensic Psychology

FORENSIC PSYCHOLOGY IS A SUBSET OF applied psychology and involves an application of clinical psychology to legal issues and investigations. It embraces studies on eyewitness identification and the determination of whether a person is a qualified witness. Because of popular television programs and movies, there is an assumption that this is associated with criminal profiling, although that is not a common career path. A person with a degree in forensic psychology would work investigating criminal activities in an effort to determine if a person was being deceptive. The goal is not to determine if a person is lying, but whether that person was being candid, which is a cautious way of indicating dishonesty. A practitioner of forensic psychology must be able to conduct investigations, develop research studies, and make assessments about the reliability of witnesses or any other people who are involved with the legal system. This would include persons of interest who may find themselves charged with a criminal act. In many criminal cases, the forensic psychologist will have to testify in court regarding the statements made by a defendant.

An example of a person who has made a career in this area is Susan Carnicero, who is the author of *Spy the Lie* and founding partner of *Qverity*. She is described as an expert in deception detection methodology and behavioral screening. This methodology is an example of the use of body language in determining if a person is being deceptive. There is a common assumption that a person who sits with folded arms is closed off and, therefore, dishonest. However, the interrogator must consider that this posture is a matter of personal comfort or the fact that the individual might simply be cold. It is essentially a self-soothing motion. Folded arms may also reflect the confidence of the person being interviewed. A skillful interrogator would avoid casual speculation based on mere assumptions. Closed posture does not always indicate deception and is usually no more than random movement.

Use of the arms can be a way in which the interviewee provides an element of protection for himself. There are specific gestures that reveal the discomfort felt by the person being questioned. Among the most common are holding some object against the chest, placing an arm in a resting position on the table, and using one arm to hold the other arm behind the back. When a person is uncomfortable, he is likely to display at least one of these behaviors. Being uncomfortable, however, does not always mean the person is deceptive. The task of the interviewer is to determine the reasons for this comfort.

The primary concern is whether the suspect's observed behavior is a direct result of the question directed to him rather than a matter of personal comfort or habit. Susan Carnicero maintains that the question is the stimulus and what you must look for is his reaction within the first five seconds. What the questioner must look for is the "timing and clusters of deceptive behavior." If the suspect does not exhibit deceptive behavior within the first five seconds, the questioner must conclude he is not lying. If, during the suspect's response to that question, there are at least one or two other instances of deceptive behavior—in other words a "cluster"—then the suspect moves into the "likely guilty" category.

It is possible that you will see a non-verbal response even before the question is completed. This is a result of the fact that a person who is speaking normally will say from 120 to 150 words a minute. By contrast, a person thinks much faster than this. Most specialists assume that human thought is ten times faster than human speech. Thought is faster because it is not expressed as words but as concepts. Therefore, you can easily have two or more non-verbal reactions—a "cluster"—almost immediately. It is important to recognize that your suspect will also exhibit some truthful behavior but that is less significant than his deceptive behavior. He does not have to lie about everything. Your focus is on his dishonest behavior. If you ask a deceptive person a question that he is comfortable answering, you will get a truthful response. It is the uncomfortable questions that tell the story.

If you imagine that you are having a discussion about a business deal rather than a criminal matter, the same assumptions apply. You ask the potential seller if this is the best price he can offer and he will try to convince you it is. This part of the interview is the time when the seller wants to show you that he is a good, honest person so you will accept his offer. What you see at this stage is your subject's effort at manipulation. In a criminal investigation this means that he wants you to accept him as an honest person. One way in which the manipulation can be seen is if, when asked about his job within an organization, he does not limit his response to "accountant" or "engineer," for example, but gives you a long statement about all of the important services he performs. This is more of his effort to convince you he is a good person. An effective interrogator will ignore truthful behavior and search for the deceptive behavior.

During this process, it is important to recognize when a person is being evasive. He will talk a lot but will avoid giving a direct response. He will speak of his service to the company but will not directly deny that he committed a crime. An honest person will be most concerned about denying guilt. The honest person will not rely on exclusionary qualifiers such as "not really," "for the most part" or "fundamentally." These qualifiers suggest that something was cut out from the complete truth. Aggression is another indication of deception. If you ask the person if he knows anything about information that has gone missing, he may respond by attacking the question and saying "you people always think I did it" whenever there is a problem. An unqualified denial of guilt would represent an honest response rather than an effort to avoid a direct response.

Another significant measure of deception is if the suspect dismisses the question as being of no importance. If he says something like "there you go again" this is a negative reaction and a possible indication of deceptive behavior. There are also non-verbal indicators that reflect

aggression. Sometimes we will see a person who smiles at an inappropriate time in the questioning. This may be a "micro" indication, but
it is highly relevant.

Again, the main point is that a suspect may talk a long time and
say he loves his murdered wife. But in all of this, he still does not
respond to the actual question, "Did you kill your wife"? The suspect
may say that he would never hurt his wife but that is different from
saying he did not hurt his wife. Conditional tense is not the same as
an explicit denial. He may talk around it in an effort to convince you
he is a good, caring person. This is an example of perception manipulation. If a person cites his strong religious beliefs in his interview, this
should be regarded as a perception qualifier. It is an effort to dress up
his lies. He will use phrases such as "to tell you the truth" or "truth-
fully." Another significant non-verbal matter is a behavioral pause. If
the pause is in response to a question about what you were doing five
years ago on this day, it is reasonable that the suspect needs time to
think. If the question is specific, such as did you rob the bank five years
ago, there is no reason for a lot of thought in considering a response.
Grooming gestures—such as fixing your hair or altering some aspect of
your clothing—are also indications of deception.

Attack behavior is another indication of deception. This does not
involve taking violent action, but is expressed as a threat, especially a
self-harm threat. Under pressure, a subject may threaten that he will
kill himself rather than continue with an interrogation. In *Spy the
Lie*, there is an account of a woman who had to be polygraphed four
times because of peculiarities of her behavior. Eventually, the applicant threatened to throw herself from the CIA's seventh floor balcony
unless the polygraph examiner backed off.

Before looking at specific interrogation techniques, it is useful to
consider something as basic as the way in which questions are formu-
lated and how subjects respond to those questions. When responding
to an interrogator's questions, it is common for the subject to make
what is called a "convincing statement." This statement is non-responsive and simply makes an assertion such as "I am not a pervert; a
pervert is the lowest form of life." With this, the subject is trying to

make the case that he is a good person but he is not denying the accusation that has been made against him. The "convincing statement" should be categorized as deceptive.

For the interrogator, the best response is to make a statement that is "below the radar" and unlikely to make the subject become defensive. A "below the radar" statement would be to agree with the convincing statement observation by saying that he is right about perverts being scum. He might add that no decent person would want to associate with a pervert. An "above the radar" statement would be a direct one, such as "I don't believe you!" With the convincing statement out of the way, the interrogator can return to direct questions about the subject's behavior.

There is one important qualification about interrogation that undermines most of the conventional techniques. If your suspect is a sociopath, the rules will change because this is a person who lacks any moral dimension. A person like Charles Manson was driven by the need to dominate, so no appeal to conscience would alter his responses. One effective approach to a sociopath is to convince him that you regard him as being completely unimportant. Otherwise, the subtleties of a conventional interrogation are lost on a person such as this.

The most important element in interrogating a psychopath is to keep them talking. Holding their interest is a challenge, so it is important to keep the discussion focused on them and to imply that you are impressed with them. Because they easily become disinterested, the interviewer is advised to be very familiar with the crime scene and the background of the psychopath. This way, they will see themselves as the main topic of the interview and that is something they find interesting. Advance preparation for an interview with a psychopath is vital. It is important to know about the psychopath's family, his arrest record, or any mental health issues in his record. Never use moral or ethical issues in appealing to the psychopath because he feels no responsibility for the consequences of his actions. There is no reason to employ emotional appeals. If the interviewer is intimately familiar with the crime scene, he might spark the genuine interest of the suspect by offering criticisms of how the crime was conducted. If the psychopath is told he made mistakes, he will be inclined to defend himself and how the crime was conducted. When the conversation is focused on this aspect of the crime, the suspect who keeps talking is likely to give up information that was previously unknown. He may eventually implicate himself. A psychopath is said to be very effective in using body language so the interviewer should pay more attention to his actual words.

Another person who is largely immune to interrogation techniques is someone who has been subjected to torture and survived. The torture survivor has sometimes developed some form of self-hypnotism that prevents them from being broken. A non-threatening form of interrogation based on the development of friendship might be the only workable approach in this case.

The same difficulties exist if the person being questioned is a professional intelligence officer. Because he has been trained to understand all of the interrogation tactics, he is difficult to trick. A "legal" intelligence officer will have a well-developed story—a legend—that he has studied extensively. Within that legend, there will be a fallback story that they can offer up as an admission of guilt but on a less significant level. If their fallback story is accepted, they will have defeated the interrogation process. An "illegal" intelligence officer like Colonel Rudolph Abel will survive by keeping a low profile. Since the legend of the "illegal" is less well-developed, it is more difficult for him to maintain his innocence.

If such a suspect has been "broken," the interrogation becomes a debriefing because the suspect has ended his evasions and will tell the truth. He may be enlisted to become a double agent. If this happens, his interrogator's role will often change and he will become the case officer and will manage the new double agent. In such a case, there will always be questions about the sincerity of the newly recruited double agent. If the double agent felt he was recruited by force it is much less likely he will be trustworthy.

Interrogating Deplorable Subjects

A T SOME POINT, EVERY INVESTIGATOR ENCOUNTERS a suspect who
is so unpleasant and detestable that the prospect of the interrogation seems unpleasant and hardly worth the effort. In this category you will encounter serial killers, mass murderers, child molesters and an assortment of deplorable individuals.

As World War II came to an end, the Nuremburg proceedings were initiated to try Nazi war criminals, including people who committed unparalleled human rights atrocities. The Allies did not want to undertake summary judgments without giving the accused a fair hearing. Therefore, they assembled judges, attorneys, witnesses and all of the experts needed in an open, fair trial.

An especially notorious figure was Hermann Goering, a political and military leader who was a senior figure in the Nazi Party and Adolph Hitler's top deputy. He was also a World War I fighter pilot as well as a participant in Hitler's 1923 coup attempt. The litany of accusations against Goering ranged from human rights violations to systematic theft of cultural treasures throughout Europe. At Nuremberg he was found guilty on four counts of war crimes and sentenced to death. However, before his sentence could be carried out in 1946, he was subjected to a long interrogation that was an effort to determine his complicity in the Nazi human rights violations. Goering's interrogation was conducted by officers of the Air POW Interrogation Detachment. In preparation for the lengthy interrogation and because of Goering's air force role, a series of questions were prepared by officers of the United States Strategic Air Forces in Europe. The interrogation was also an attempt to develop a comprehensive account of

German wartime activities that would help in preparing a history of general developments during the Nazi period.

There were specific topics relating to air power of the Allies, the Germans, the Japanese and the Italians. Interrogators also wanted details of the Battle of Britain and the Russian campaign. The interrogations, all of which were recorded, explored questions about the extent to which Adolph Hitler dictated Luftwaffe policy and micro-managed the German air campaign. At one point, Goering observed that Hitler was a "great ally" of the United States and Britain in matters of aerial warfare. He insisted that the Luftwaffe could have easily defeated Britain without a land invasion had Hitler not diverted so much of Germany's assets to the campaign against Russia. He was also critical of Italy and declared that Germany would have fared better if Italy had joined the Allies. One of the most important lines of questioning was the effort to study how strategic decisions affected how the Germans used air power. This included an examination of German progress in the development of new airplanes. Goering suggested that if they had enjoyed just four additional months on such work, the tide of the war could have changed. Finally, while not as important in the area of human rights violations, the Allies wanted to learn about the disposition of the art treasures taken by many Nazi leaders, especially Goering, in an effort to return those cultural treasures to their rightful owners.

More troubling is the interrogation of people seen as traitors. For the British, there were several people who fell into the category, few more notorious or despicable than the US-born Briton William Joyce known as "Lord Haw Haw" to his radio listeners. In a sneering, upper class manner, he broadcast Nazi propaganda to the UK throughout the war and even took German citizenship in 1940. While living in Britain, he had been associated with the Black and Tans, a group of constables who fought against Irish nationalists. The Black and Tans were known as a terrorist group and when Joyce was only 14, he participated in the murder of an Irish priest. As an adult, Joyce became deputy leader of the British Union of Fascists but was so violent that he was expelled from the organization. The main issue during his short interrogation was that he had never been a British subject. However, when he was found to be in possession of an illegal British passport, authorities cited that as justification for his trial. He was convicted and hanged on January 3, 1946.

Another deplorable subject was the serial killer Richard Ramirez who in 1985 was charged with 14 counts of murder, two kidnappings, seven rapes, and three lewd acts with children, as well as myriad robberies and burglaries. He was better known as the "Night Stalker," and his murderous actions terrorized residents of Los Angeles. His ultimate capture was facilitated by an angry crowd that held him until police arrived. The attorneys for Ramirez complained that his requests for legal representation were ignored by police, who threatened to charge him with more crimes if he did not talk to them.

According to Ramirez's interrogators, the greatest success came when using an approach based on respect and an avoidance of being judgmental. He was described as being open and having a good sense of humor. In his responses, Ramirez made much of the fact that he was a Satanist and would elaborate on his philosophy about death. He felt that death should be regarded as a spiritual thing rather than viewed simply in medical or scientific terms. He suggested that by ignoring the spiritual aspects of death, contemporary society had diminished the meaning of life. He often referred to the so-called "death rattle" made by people as they die and described it as a spasm of the voice box. In his view, any person who did not hear that was simply not focused on reality.

One of the topics to which Ramirez repeatedly referred during his interrogations was the impact of Satanism on his life. He had grown up as a Christian, but by the time he was 17 or 18, he came to believe nothing. It was not until two or three years later when a person he met in jail told him about Satan that he became what he viewed as a Satanist. He described Satanism as a "stabilizing force" in his life that gave him a reason for living. Once he heard about Satan he devoted himself to reading books about Satan and studying how Satan would direct his life. He compared his situation to that of terrorist groups that were motivated by their religious beliefs. Ramirez pointed out that even members of the drug cartels such as Adolfo Constanzo, who made human sacrifices to pagan gods, believed that Satan provided protection.

While Ramirez did not claim to be a warlock or someone who knew Satanism "from A to Z," he did focus on the rituals associated with Satanism. Going into court, he showed news cameras his hand with a Pentagram drawn in his palm. He explained that he did this to show he was allied with Satan. Although he was enthusiastic about Satanism, he warned those who interviewed him that caution should be used in trying to summon an evil spirit because failure to use the correct ritual or summoning the wrong demons could result in death.

In his efforts to understand Satanism and the minds of people who enjoyed inflicting pain, Ramirez studied the Marquis de Sade and discussed his case and the motivations of such a person. More than that, Ramirez used his speculations about the Marquis de Sade to help cultivate an image for what increasingly became his public. He could be very charismatic and enjoyed giving interviews so people could see him as a charming person.

His charming persona was apparently a factor in eluding the police until he was caught racing through a red light while driving a stolen car as he escaped from a crime scene. The officer who stopped him asked if he was a serial killer. Ramirez, as he scratched a Pentagram on the hood of his car, made a prayer to Satan, and smiled at the officer. When the officer inquired again if he was sure he was not a serial killer, Ramirez jumped a fence and ran away. The policeman, assuming he was simply a typical local lunatic, made little effort to pursue Ramirez and did not call for backup assistance.

In his interrogations, Ramirez described serial killers in terms of the victims they sought. For police, the first suspects in a conventional murder are the acquaintances or family members of the victims. A spouse is generally the first person to be interrogated by police. In a serial killer case, police have the challenge of investigating a case in which a stranger was killed by a stranger. Thus, they are denied the first, obvious step in their investigation. What remains at that point is an effort to identify common characteristics of the victims. Among the most common victims are prostitutes, homeless people, and young boys. None of these avenues offer good leads in the early days of an investigation.

Detecting Truth When Dealing
With the Occult

IN RECENT YEARS THERE HAVE BEEN numerous killings associated with Satanists. For investigators, this phenomenon creates a special set of circumstances. In 2017, a 35-year-old North Carolina man was arrested for the murder of two men who were found buried in his back yard. Police reported that the walls of the man's home were covered in Pentagrams, animal feces, and drawings of the devil. His wife, who was also charged, described herself as a Satanist, as did his mother, who lived in the same house. The group routinely practiced Satanic rituals and animal sacrifices. The challenge during interrogations was that the suspects either refused to speak at all or when they did they made contradictory statements.

In 2019, an Oklahoma teenager, who had believed his parents were Satan worshippers who communicated with him telepathically, killed both parents. Afterwards, he was non-responsive during police interrogations and would not speak with his attorney. This behavior constituted the basis for the attorney's non-guilty by reason of insanity plea and his argument that the youth was not fit to stand trial.

As noted above, how people respond during an interrogation is a product of their culture. Cultural factors encourage many people to respond directly and freely. Other cultures have an opposite impact and the subject of an interview is consistently recalcitrant. The dominant culture in the United States is western and reflects values shaped by a largely Christian tradition. The emergence of counter-cultures undermines the western outlook and can create difficulties for interrogators. Equally important is the challenge that civilians face in determining the honesty of people they encounter. While that may not be an issue for law enforcement, it is a problem for citizens trying to protect their personal, professional, and financial interests.

Richard Ramirez's interviewers—whether police officers or journalists—became aware of this. They remarked on the extent to which Satanism shaped his worldview and his attitudes about the crimes he committed. Interrogators are trained to search for motives when confronting a suspect. Because of his Satanic beliefs, his motives were difficult to evaluate.

In recent years, there has been an increase in the numbers of people claiming to follow Satan and worshipping in Satanic churches. Police officers in India have documented difficulties in interrogating such individuals because they don't accept the concept of murder but insist the killer has simply freed the victim from human bondage. In 2017, authorities reported on a case involving a 30-year-old Cadell Jeanson Raja who confessed to murdering four family members with an ax. Raja seemed delusional when the interrogation began. He made no effort to escape but was not at all remorseful. In fact, he proudly boasted that he had "freed" his family members. According to police, he was obsessed with the occult and claimed to have used *astral projection*—which is part of the local form of Satan worship—in accomplishing the murders. Within Hindu culture, there are three kinds of astral projection. In the first kind, the subject uses deep meditation to reach the astral plane. The second is spontaneous astral projection or Out of Body Experience. The final one is unconscious and takes place while the subject is asleep. This avenue offers the best plea for avoiding conviction. The logic behind this conception is that it helps explain the suspect's motive and that it will shape the investigation process.

In India, Satanic practices often have a great impact on police investigations because so many of them involve breaking laws. The Satanic black mass requires the desecration of consecrated hosts that must be stolen from Catholic churches. There is now a lucrative market for selling consecrated hosts to be used in black masses. Cult leaders desecrate the host by defecating or urinating on it. A human skull is used for drinking impure blood during the black masses which are held each month on the 13th day. During their services, the cults use pagan occult symbols and recite Christian hymns backwards.

Gangs use the Satanic groups as a way of marketing drugs used in the black masses. These services also can involve the abuse of small children, and a few years ago eleven Indian Satanists were arrested for abusing young children over a period of years. Police interrogations in these crimes have been hampered by worshippers' use of ritualistic practices to avoid giving information. Those same practices are useful in deceiving the unwary targets of cult members.

Kerela's commercial capital of Kochi is the main center for Satanic cults in India. Their growth took place as the tourist trade in Fort Kochi began to develop in 2000. It was French tourists whose visits provided a source for money needed to develop the cults. It was with great difficulty that local police were able to trace their funding operations to crimes involving the tourists. By using isolated or abandoned houses, the cults now operate churches in seven out of the fourteen districts in Kerela.

These operations have become profitable by promising to help people with their struggling businesses. They promise fortunes while destroying enemies. In order to join in the Black Masses, participants pay as much as $30,000. Many people are drawn to the cults by the prospect of some form of sacrilegious sex or the availability of illegal drugs. There is a Hindu cult that makes similar offers and uses black arts for people needing relief from their sufferings. They worship an avatar of Vishnu, a vengeful god who rides a buffalo. Every Friday there is an animal sacrifice after which the priest will meet with people to tell them how much of an offering they must make in order to receive specific benefits.

These Satanic temples advertise in newspapers and on television. By making extravagant promises they have accumulated massive fortunes and are able to start large businesses. Police complain that under current laws, they can only prosecute when someone reports how they might have been damaged or defrauded by the cults. Since many people are afraid of them, they are reluctant to lodge complaints and police investigations usually stall in the early days. It is essentially scam artists who prey on tourists, locals, or people looking for an easy answer to their problems.

We expect Satanic cults to appear in large cities where there are more potential victims and a bigger community in which to hide. Research, however, shows that they can be found in a wide variety of settings. There are many unlikely locations that have an association with Satanic practices. However, an association should not be seen as something that is genuinely sinister. Often it is merely sensationalism promoted for thrill seeking adolescents or con artists.

Because of the commercial success of the 1977 book *The Amityville Horror* and the subsequent movie, the town of Amityville, New York became a mecca for people hoping to experience a chill by being in that infamous location. There is no doubt that in 1974, Ronald "Butch" DeFeo, Jr. killed six family members. However, most people do not take seriously his claim that devilish black hands and disembodied voices ordered him to do this. It did create a good horror story and a popular movie. For later owners hoping to sell the house, it was an effective sales gimmick. Over the years, this legend has served as a key element in duping people and often making money. Even if a person did not believe the stories around the residence, it always made for an exciting story.

The Staten Island region has an occult association that is much more than the Amityville story. This association began with the urban legend of Cropsey, a man who had been horribly burned and placed in a mental hospital. Cropsey was rumored to have become a homicidal maniac who roamed the area looking for the children who burned him. While this story was not true, it did give local parents a legend to frighten their children with if they did not behave. In the 1980s, a homeless man who lived in an abandoned building on the island attacked several children. The man was eventually caught and this story became a horror movie. The fact that there was a local congregation of the Church of Satan contributed to the proliferation of stories based on some version of the Cropsey legend.

When a family that was attempting to recover from a personal tragedy moved to the area in 2006, they claimed that their home was haunted. They spoke of seeing hooded men in the yard and hearing ghostly voices in the house. When they discovered the diary of a young girl who had lived there in 1927, the rumors intensified. The diary was an account of Satanic rituals such as animal sacrifice being practiced in the house. The family continued to experience the hauntings and eventually a television program—Paranormal Witness—aired their story. With this level of attention, many locals continue to express a strong belief that the entire area is haunted.

Another location that has occult connections is Fort Thomas, Kentucky, a small city with a population of just over 16,000. Its notoriety stems from the 1896 murder of a pregnant woman named Pearl Bryan. Her headless body was found on a local farm, and police apprehended the two killers who claimed to be practicing occultists. Until the time of their executions, they refused to tell interrogators what they had done with her head. Both men explained that if they gave up this information, they would face the wrath of the devil in the afterlife.

The first public Satanic group in the United States appeared in Toledo, Ohio in 1948. This was the Our Lady of Endor Coven which was started by Herbert Arthur Sloane. Black magic rituals were performed by Sloane in the back room of the barber shop he ran. The Our Lady of Endor Coven was a branch of a Gnostic religious organization known as the Ophite Cultus Sathanas. Sloane claimed the devil appeared to him when he was a child and returned when Sloane was 25 years old. Because his approach to Satanism was largely mystical or cerebral without the lurid trappings of later groups, it did not have widespread appeal and remained rather small.

The best-known location for Satanic associations is San Francisco. Anton Szandor LaVey's Church of Satan, which appeared 20 years after Sloane's Our Lady of Endor Coven, is the center for the occult not only in San Francisco but also throughout much of the United States. When LaVey's *The Satanic Bible* was published in 1969, it became an important recruiting tool for Satanic groups. Richard Ramirez cited it as an important influence on his decision to embrace Satanism. LaVey had an eclectic background and had worked as a crime scene photographer, a night club musician, a lion tamer, and psychic. He started his church in 1966 and used his massive haunted-looking black home as the place for the dramatic rituals associated with the church. Several Hollywood celebrities such as Sammy Davis, Jr. joined the church and the criminal activities of the Zodiac Killer and Richard Ramirez enhanced San Francisco's image as a center of the occult.

In recent years, Satanic organizations accustomed to hiding from public view have made their way into public debates about religious freedom. In 2017, the city council in Belle Plaine, Minnesota approved plans to erect a Satanic monument in the "free speech" area of the town park. This project was sponsored by a Satanic temple, based in Salem, Massachusetts, and a local religious freedom group. When the council announced its decision, there was an outpouring of public opposition. In order to end the controversy, the council simply eliminated the "free speech" area of the park, thus killing the plan for a Satanic monument.

Popular images of the occult or of the Church of Satan focus on the sinister aspects of what is seen as devil worship. A Richard Ramirez helps cultivate such an image. It is not surprising, therefore, that advocates of modernization and, perhaps, marketing, are developing a more "modern" form of Satanism. This approach essentially transforms Satanism into a self-help methodology coupled with gluttony that can direct its followers toward personal and professional satisfaction. It is no longer based simply on a rejection of Catholicism.

Much of the literature of the modern Church of Satan is organized around "success stories" of young people who have embraced the values of this new faith. Its philosophy is drawn from the ideas of Friedrich Nietzsche and Ayn Rand and its dogma is not based on worshipping an external force but on worshipping oneself. The modern Satanist does not deny our carnal instincts but teaches that each person needs to find a safe way to indulge in them. He rejects traditional religion as mass-market consumerism while Satanism is about developing one's personal abilities. By comparison with the visions of Satanism as a sinister faith that embodies animal worship and casting spells, the modern Satanism seems rather bland and more like the advice found in books on the self-help aisle in a bookstore. Nonetheless, spokesmen claim as evidence of their success the fact that their Twitter account has 214,000 followers while the Twitter account of the Church of England has a mere 87,000 followers.

There are uses of Satanism that are not at all like the relatively saccharin self-help philosophy espoused in modern publications. In fact, it has been used to advance business interests without invoking spells or demons. One of the most notorious cases of using an accusation of Satanism to undermine a business rival was the Satanic Panic of 1982 in which rumors circulated that the Proctor and Gamble company was a front for devil worship. In the 1970s and 1980s, there were rumors that Satanism was spreading across the country. The popularity of movies like *The Exorcist,* occult-themed songs such as "Don't Fear the Reaper," and lurid accounts of the Manson Family helped drive these fears. The P&G logo, an image featuring a face in a moon looking at 13 stars which represented the original 13 colonies, was created in 1930 but did not draw critical attention until the 1980s. The original accusation was leveled by a man named Jim Peters, who was associated with the Zion Christian Life Center in St. Paul, Minnesota. The first reaction of P&G management was to ignore these peculiar accusations, rather than give them more attention than they deserved. Their assumption was that if someone wanted to believe such a story, there was not much that could be done to prevent that. The popular Phil Donahue talk show even did an episode about this controversy.

While Jim Peters went on to other causes, the story reappeared in 1982 and contained specifics that were not provided in the 1980 account. Although nonsensical, much was made that the beard on the figure in the moon looked a lot like the number six. Moreover, the curls were in a pattern of three sixes which were said to indicate the mark of the beast—666. P&G adopted an aggressive public relations campaign and filed a series of lawsuits against anyone pushing this narrative. They also withdrew the logo which had been the spark for the rumors. The P&G efforts were productive and the Satanic story was gone by the end of the year.

Unfortunately, the story returned in 1985 when someone distributed thousands of leaflets in New York City. The leaflets maintained outrageously that P&G was actually in league with the devil. Eventually, leaflets were sent to numerous small churches in the south and the Midwest. Many people accepted the accusations as true and spread the word to others. P&G employees would be confronted by relatives who feared they were working with devil worshippers. In 1986, the South Dakota Attorney General was forced to issue a statement explaining that there was no proof that P&G officials were working with the devil.

In 1990, more lawsuits were filed over this accusation, but there was now an identifiable target—Amway—a minor business rival to P&G. Amway distributors used their company voicemail system to charge that P&G profits were being used to fund the Church of Satan. In 1995, the Amway campaign was reignited and more P&G lawsuits followed. These civil suits were an effective, albeit costly, weapon that took over a decade to resolve in court.

Amway officials maintained that Proctor and Gamble was not able to demonstrate that they suffered any financial losses because of the Satan worshipping story. In 2003, the US Circuit Court of Appeals in Denver agreed with Amway's contention that the rumors were not defamatory and that P&G had failed to show evidence of specific financial damages. P&G was able to get the case reinstated and a jury awarded them over $19 million in a civil lawsuit. Four Amway distributors were charged with spreading rumors linking P&G to Satanism in order to enhance their profits. While pleased with this victory, P&G spokesmen suggested their main concern was not money, but their company's reputation. The P&G logo was restored in 2013.

Satanist groups are not working to gain support from corporations such as Proctor and Gamble and there is no evidence to support the contention that any corporations share the "Satanic agenda." The overall objective of Satanic groups is to gain mainstream acceptance. They want to benefit from American concepts of religious freedom and have a presence on the public square along with Baptists, Methodists, and every other religion or denomination.

There is a clear dichotomy in the character of the groups pushing this agenda. The first is the dark Satanists who practice frightening rituals and alienate so many Americans. The second group is the moderate or enlightened Satanists who benefit from the extreme positions and macabre rituals of the dark Satanists. These Satanists claim that they do not worship Satan at all but merely use him for a shocking symbol that will attract neutral readers. An example of one of the churches in the group of enlightened Satanists is the Satanic Temple, which targets elementary schools by trying to set up After School Satan Clubs to compete with any Christian groups that might be in the school. The Satanic Temple often petitions to erect Satanic statues next to any Christian monument.

By contrast, there are some Satanic groups that are more aggressive and use public ridicule of the Catholic mass as a tactic. They try to organize the Black Mass as a caricature of the Catholic Mass. In Oklahoma City, a group organized a blasphemous and sacrilegious ceremony on the sidewalk directly in front of a Catholic Church on Christmas Eve. Satanists do not expect such events to bring in multitudes of new followers. Their actual goal is broader: they want public acceptance of Satanism as normal and an acceptable alternative to Catholics or Protestants. This means they have to do things to keep the idea of Satan in the news as a topic of routine discussion.

The persistence of occult beliefs and their recent transformations raise questions about our perceptions. It also places new demands on our ability to resist deceptive presentations that may create problems that are more relevant for how people see the world. It is a variation on the con man schemes to sell the Brooklyn Bridge or the Eiffel Tower. Though it can be associated with horrible crimes, it has a marginal impact on law enforcement. However, it can be a devastating life altering force for the lives of those who accept its practices.

It has become apparent that we live in a world where there is almost no expectation of privacy. Therefore, other techniques have been employed. A useful term that describes the way in which communication can be made virtually incomprehensible in order to mislead people is obfuscation. The use of technical jargon and confusing or ambiguous language helps accomplish this objective. Obfuscation is intentional when the objective is to mislead the listener. Or it may be unintentional simply because of poorly written or verbal presentations. Obfuscation can also be a way of talking around the main point of a conversation as a means of hiding the explicit meaning from an unwanted listener. This is often referred to as security through obscurity. It is deliberate but should not be associated with conduct intended to take advantage of the unwary. People who are worried about surveillance teams might employ obfuscation. Those hoping to dodge something as mundane as social media algorithms that would ban your conversation will employ this technique. This is not an explicit example of lying but it does demonstrate the subtleties of deception.

Interrogations, Identity and General Observations

THERE ARE VARIOUS TYPES OF INTERROGATIONS, but the selection of a specific type must be a function of the nature of the investigation it is to support. If the target of the investigation is thought to be a spy, there will be a set of complications requiring not only questioning but extensive research. The basic task of determining who the suspect is brings an assortment of challenges. This is much more than a mere identity check. The fact that a person can show apparently valid documents does not tell you who that person really is. Documents can always be fabricated even in our age of sophisticated technologies. Going beyond this requires a detailed process known as backgrounding, something that is not associated with criminal investigations. Through backgrounding it is possible to determine if you are dealing with a real person who can be identified, rather than a social fiction created by digital deceptions.

If you encounter a childhood friend, someone you have known since you were in kindergarten, it is possible that your lives have moved in different directions in terms of professions, education, and family circumstances. You may find that you no longer have common interests or experiences. When you get beyond discussing your elementary school teachers, the discussion will end. You no longer know each other and your old friend is now a stranger. One purpose of the special background investigation is to explore those experiences and associations that make you who you are and distinguish you from who you used to be.

Backgrounding explores the historical dimension of the individual.

You as an adult are no longer the person you might have been as a teenager because identity is constantly evolving. As an adult, you would not want to be evaluated on the basis of you the high school student. The immature qualities you exhibited in high school will likely be dormant in you the adult. An identity can be manufactured but for it to have reality, there are certain characteristics that must adhere to an individual. One of those characteristics might be a commitment to an ideology or loyalty to the state. These are matters that require a prolonged investigation which will not be easily completed by the collection of mere documents. Because a human being can have many identities, the investigator must determine which identity is still embraced by a particular person. In order to determine the suspect's loyalty, the investigator must sift through a mountain of facts—both relevant and irrelevant—to determine if he has caught a spy.

There are numerous components of human identity that must be examined as part of the process of a background investigation. It would start with the person's name. In many societies, there is a belief that if someone knows your real name, they possess part of your soul. Therefore, in such societies, people are reluctant to share the complete real name. A name can even tell part of your history in the manner of long Spanish names that indicate the various families in your background. As an example, the name Pablo Picasso is concise and generally used to identify the artist. However, his complete name— Pablo Diego José Francisco de Paula Juan Nepomuceno María de los Remedios Cipriano de la Santísima Trinidad Ruiz y Picasso—tells a story about his background and family.

Another ingredient of a human identity is physical appearance. When we say we recognize a person, it is usually because of their appearance even though we know that appearances change. A class reunion reminds us of this fact. We become fatter, grayer, and wrinkled with age. Ethnicity is one of the ingredients of human identity. Skin pigmentation, physiognomy, and language are common functions of ethnicity.

Personal characteristics also help us identify people. Some characteristics are more difficult than others to alter. Age is an important characteristic and there are limits to how a person might hide their age. Debilitating infirmities, such as a missing limb or a pronounced limp, are characteristics that often make a person stand out in a crowd.

An intangible component of identity is our personal history. This is something that has an indelible impact on the person to whom it belongs. While many elements of personal history can be faked, there are parts of it that can never be obscured. A person who was confined for years in a concentration camp or a Soviet gulag will always behave in a distinctive manner that may facilitate his identification. Sometimes this is something that is subtle, like reactions to certain situations or people, but it will always be present.

Experience, while part of one's personal history, also helps forge an identity. It is different from our personal history because it is usually shared with other people. This means that one way of studying your identity is to interview people with whom you served in some capacity. A suspect may deny having been to a certain place but if he traveled there with others, their accounts undermine the suspect's denial. A denial may not be intentionally deceptive, but could be a response to a traumatic event.

Our achievements are an important part of who we are. A person who acquires various academic qualifications will be changed by those accomplishments. Someone with a classical education will be different from who he was before being educated. That education will have an impact on how he speaks or how he treats others. He may become arrogant or he might learn the importance of humility. Achievements represent mile markers as we go through life and claims that a person makes can be verified or disproved by an examination of their achievement. A forty year old person who claims to have climbed the Matterhorn in 1985 is obviously lying because we calculate that he was a small child in that year.

Our connections with other people represent links that prove an individual was part of a particular community. A spy who claims that he grew up in Vienna, Austria will be able to verify that claim if he can cite individuals with whom he socialized. He will have a certain accent and mannerisms. A claim to be a product of Vienna will not be credible if investigators are unable to locate any of the person's classmates or neighbors.

Relationships to things are another component of identity. Most people accumulate things as they go through life. These material possessions need not be of any great value but they do indicate the identity of a person. We collect things. It may be theatre tickets, stamps, or books. Memorabilia mark our existence in certain places or environments and in most homes you will see things on display. The home of a retired Navy officer will be cluttered with various items that remind him of places he served or visited. You can stroll through the house of a complete stranger and learn a lot by observing possessions he has accumulated. Those material possessions help define who we are. A person who sets out to disappear will always be reminded to develop totally different interests to cement his new identity.

Finally, memories are a vital indication of a person's identity. These are not things that can be put on display in the den, but they shape who the person is. Memories cause certain types of behavior. People who spent years in a Soviet prison recount that once they got out, they followed certain rituals. Many had a lifelong tendency to hide food because of their memories of hunger while in prison camps. Memories may be triggered by sights, sounds, or smells and when encountering them, the person's behavior will change accordingly. Those memories demonstrate connections to that person's identity.

None of this is helpful in and of itself. Detecting or identifying intent requires the investigator—or any interested observer—to understand culture and context. To acquire intimate familiarity with a new environment, an interrogator needs extensive training. This can be conducted in field training if he can spend time in the relevant country but there are now numerous computer games to facilitate training. In order to identify anomalous behavior, it is essential to understand what constitutes a behavioral norm. In other words, how should a person from a particular background behave when he is being truthful? When using modern screening programs in airports and train stations, there will still be numerous false-positive identifications. To guard against this, security personnel must employ both technology and sophisticated interview techniques. This is a situation in which certain aspects of body language, especially facial micro-expressions, would be useful.

An act of espionage is less likely to be witnessed by individuals outside an intelligence facility or some place that contains sensitive information relating to national security. This does not mean that investigators do not interview neighbors and coworkers but there is less expectation that these interviews will produce the "smoking gun" that can be introduced as evidence in court.

If there is an investigation in the area of industrial espionage, it may be somewhat less complex than espionage relating to national security. Various countries, as well as companies, devote considerable attention to stealing proprietary information. Russian budgets routinely cited theft in calculating the cost of developing a product. This was not exceptional but was listed in budgetary spread sheets. Industrial espionage can be facilitated by identifying a vulnerable employee or by having the spy attempt to gain employment in the target industry. Intelligence organizations such as the East German Stasi trained agents to meet employees in the target industry who might be vulnerable because of personal debts or loneliness. Less systematic but at least more simple is the tactic of entering the target facility when it is closed and searching for the information that is needed. The capacity of cell phones and other small devices gives industrial espionage agents an advantage.

For investigators, the key is to keep meticulous records of what individuals have access to sensitive information. If something has gone missing, this is the first place to look. It is vital to determine what information is sensitive and might be targeted by a rival industry or a foreign power. A risk assessment program should identify weaknesses in the company's facility. This includes cyber vulnerabilities that could make it possible for an intruder to get into the company's computer system and drain valuable data. The objectives of embezzlement investigation share certain common features. The first is to determine if there has actually been a theft of company property. The second is to calculate the total value of lost assets. And, finally, you want to remove dishonest employees and recover the losses associated with the crime.

The investigative plan should have certain specific features. Making a list of all employees that had relevant access as well as capabilities for the theft is essential. In preparing this list, do not take into account length of service or position within the firm. It is often those that enjoy the greatest wealth who want even more. In the early days of the investigation, do not be confrontational or accusative in approaching possible suspects. Doing this will simply create a toxic environment and undermine investigative efforts.

Economic crimes such as embezzlement carry their own set of complexities. They are among the most complex of workplace investigations and generally require the enlistment of forensic accountants and data retrieval experts. It is in the field of forensic accounting that we find the main investigators for this type of crime. Such an investigation must begin with an identification of a financial loss and how it took place. One problem with embezzlement is that it could occur for years without being discovered. It is not like a straightforward robbery like when the thieves come through the door brandishing weapons. Because embezzlers often destroy records in order to hide evidence that a crime has occurred, the first step is to check that all company records are in place. It is also important to look for inconsistencies in accounting records. If there are unexplained imbalances, these should be taken as a clue that embezzlement has occurred. Finally, mistakes will always be made where humans are responsible for making payments. However, if auditors find an unusual number of errors, such as duplicate payments or even altered checks, it is likely beyond a matter of simple human error, and is likely a deliberate campaign to divert funds from the company accounts.

In an economic or embezzlement case, investigators should pay attention to the suspect's behavior. Governmental agencies such as the CIA now take into account the economic circumstances of employees. In fact, any institution that deals with items of economic value—be it cash or items of value—needs to be aware of employees facing economic difficulties. That could mean employees living beyond their means, such as the spy Aldrich Ames, or those who seem worried about their finances. Work habits may be revealing, as when an employee keeps odd hours, always coming in early or working very late. Their motive could be a desire to be in the office when others are not there as this makes theft easier to accomplish. An embezzler is less likely to take time off and will let his leave time accumulate. His motive may be a reluctance to leave the office and allow others pick up some of his responsibilities. There could be a danger that during an absence someone might discover suspicious details in his work. Finally, you should be suspicious if a person always wants to work alone and won't accept help from others. Such behavior could indicate that he has something to hide. Once the thief and his method of embezzlement have been identified, the final step is to perform a risk assessment. This is a necessary part of working to prevent future losses.

If the investigation relates to a conventional criminal action such as bank robbery, there will be a greater reliance on witness testimony and surveillance cameras. There will be an examination of photographs held by the police as an effort to identify a suspect. These procedures are complex and well developed. They will be examined below.

Interrogating Saddam Hussein

OPERATION DESERT SPIDER, THE PROGRAM FOR interrogating Saddam Hussein, began in December 2003 following his capture. High Value Detainee #1, as Saddam was identified by US personnel, was found by the troops who had been looking for him since Iraq's defeat hiding in a "spider hole." The first step of Operation Desert Spider was to determine exactly what issues should be covered. In a general sense, questions focused on his political career from his role in the 1959 coup attempt to the final days of his regime. Interrogators were interested in the Iran–Iraq War and the use of chemical weapons during that conflict. There was a great need for information about Iraq's weapons of mass destruction program and the country's remaining military capability. A special concern was to understand why Saddam had blocked UN inspectors from evaluating his weapons program. He insisted that he blocked inspectors because he did not want the Iranians to learn details and weaknesses of Iraq's WMD program.

Since the invasion of Iraq had been justified by (false) suggestions that there had been a close relationship between Iraq and al-Qaeda, it was important to question Saddam about this. Throughout his interrogation, he denied that he cooperated with al-Qaeda and dismissed Osama bin Laden a "zealot."

From the first days after Saddam's capture, there was reluctance by many agencies to accept responsibility for interrogating him. While "success," however defined, could make a career, "failure" could just as easily destroy it. The interrogation began with the US Army Military Intelligence Corps. Their interrogators felt that Saddam was being evasive in his responses. Each session began with Saddam demanding that his interrogators identify themselves and their official positions. The CIA considered this prospect but feared that if Saddam went to trial, the CIA interrogators might end up having to testify in court. Ultimately, most of the responsibility fell to the FBI, which selected an Assyrian American supervisory special agent named George Piro. One of the qualifications that called for his selection was that he was one of the few FBI officials who fluently spoke Arabic. The FBI was a logical agency choice because FBI agents are skilled in interrogating suspects who will have to face legal prosecution.

The formal "interviews" began on 7 February 2004 and were conducted in secret. Since Saddam faced the prospect of the death penalty, officials feared that he had little incentive to provide information. When the CIA was considering taking the lead in the interrogation, they intended to use multiple interrogators and to possibly employ the "good cop/bad cop" routine. The FBI concluded that it was going to be necessary to develop rapport with Saddam. Therefore, George Piro was to be the only interrogator and, over a long period of time, was able to develop rapport with the prisoner. Enhanced interrogation methods, which were favored by the CIA, were rejected by the FBI because they were both against FBI policy and were seen as likely to be ineffective.

At his first meeting with Piro, Saddam confronted the young FBI agent about his age. Being prepared, Piro replied by pointing out that when Saddam reached his first powerful political position, he was one year younger than Piro. When he initiated the interrogation process, he felt that psychological tactics might be effective and required Saddam to be seated with his back to the wall. His idea was to have total control over every aspect of Saddam's situation in order to make him dependent on his interrogator. Eventually, he decided that one of the best tactics was to let Saddam feel that he was still important and would be treated with respect. No matter how long Saddam talked, Piro would listen patiently. He was not allowed to make threats or give a promise of better treatment in return for cooperation as this was counter to FBI policy and, more importantly, would not have been helpful.

John Nixon's book *Debriefing the President* provides some interesting insights into the interrogation of Saddam Hussein. Nixon, a CIA analyst at the time, was involved with the interrogation process in its earlier days. According to Nixon, the important advantage in questioning Saddam was that he "loved to talk, especially about himself." Therefore, if you were willing to listen, he could be an excellent interview subject. Moreover, Saddam was genuinely proud of his accomplishments as the president of Iraq and wanted to tell people about them. For Nixon, Saddam's body language was not a useful clue in determining the truthfulness of his statements. In fact, he said when observing Saddam's body language he was inclined to suspect that he was dishonest when, he later learned, Saddam was being truthful.

One general objective of the interrogation was to study the construct of Saddam's regime and to examine his leadership methods. With time, it became apparent that Saddam still seemed to possess the qualities required to run Iraq, and he retained his swagger, believing he was still the rightful president. Nixon believed that Saddam's interest in the Americans was just as great as the American interest in him. He would constantly ask about his questioners' interests and backgrounds. If Saddam had any sort of hidden agenda it was probably to divert guilt from himself and to avoid discouraging the continuing resistance to the American occupation.

The interrogation also revealed that while Saddam clearly understood the politics and culture of Iraq he was relatively naïve about international affairs. He was surprised by the American reaction to his invasion of Kuwait, believing the US would understand his need to cross his southern border. Even worse was his miscalculation about the impact of the September 11 terrorist attacks. He believed the attacks would actually draw the United States and Iraq closer together in opposition to radical Islamic movements that threatened the interests of both countries. Saddam expressed his confusion about inconsistencies in US foreign policy and did not understand why Washington supported Iraq in the early 1980s but denounced the country as being a Hitler-type aggressor a decade later. More recently, there was confusion about the role of Muqtada al-Sadr, the Shia cleric and militia leader, who was denounced by President George W. Bush as being a thug that was worse than Saddam. For his part, Saddam appeared confused by the intricacies of American policy.

Interrogations for National Security

ARGUABLY THE MOST EFFECTIVE INTERROGATION TECHNIQUE is non-confrontational. Using this method enables the questioner to avoid denigrating or threatening the subject. The general assumption of non-confrontational questioning is that you are having a conversation with your subject and hope to win him over to a state in which he will confess or give you the needed information. This may well be especially effective in an interrogation involving national security concerns. But what is most apparent is that a national security interrogation can be overwhelmingly complex and based on a consideration of whether or not the enemy knows what you know. It illustrates the significance of being able to perpetrate an important lie as opposed to the sort of trivial lie told by a celebrity being quoted on TMZ.

There are interrogation techniques—often referred to as Deep Interrogation—that are illegal. While many of these were developed by the British, numerous other regimes have employed them. Most accounts of prisoners being held in the Soviet Union mention prolonged wall-standing as something employed by the NKVD and later by the KGB. Hooding is another technique that is often employed in counter-terrorist operations and it has been practiced around the world over several centuries. During the US military operation in Panama in 1989, US forces subjected their main target, Manuel Noriega, to loud rap music, something that was especially repugnant to the classical music lover. In fact, the use of any kind of noise is generally prohibited; sleep deprivation is something which is extremely disorienting after a long period of time. While associated with both the Nazis and the Soviets, this illegal practice is still widely used. Finally, deprivation of food and water is another prohibited practice which seems almost universal among dictatorial states.

Deception is another important interrogation technique. If an interrogator hopes to obtain a confession from the suspect, it can be very effective to suggest that someone else has already implicated him. A suspect who believes that the case against him has been proven is more likely to confess. There are no regulations that would prevent an interrogator from using lies to elicit a confession. Indeed, the Supreme Court has ruled that police are permitted to lie to a suspect to secure a confession.

Another tool that might be used for counter intelligence purposes is known as the Stroop effect. This effect or test was named after John Ridley Stroop who wrote about it in 1935. The Stroop effect is a neuropsychological test has been used as a way of examining the psychological capacities of test subjects during the 20th century. It is based on an assumption that certain people associate words with particular colors. In this test, subjects must view a chart on which words are written in different colors. If the word "red" appears it may be written in green. The test participant is required to say the written word and ignore the color. In order to see the relevance of the Stroop effect for investigatory purposes, there is an account that illustrates its use. Presumably, a suspected Russian spy is being interrogated. He denies that he is a spy and claims he has no knowledge of the Russian language. The interrogation team used the Stroop test in Russian. When the subject saw the word "yellow" written in blue he hesitated and responded by saying "blue" when he should have said "yellow." The testers' assumption was that this constituted proof he actually knew the Russian language.

There are innumerable tactics employed by interrogators, as well as by individuals hoping to resist interrogation. One of the traditional tactics employed by the Abwehr during World War II was the "built in flaw" in an agent's story. By creating a flaw that could be detected by the interrogator, the suspect could confess to this flaw in his story and, hopefully, convince the interrogator that he is stupid, but not actually a spy. For example, the spy's story might be that he worked as a lawyer when, in fact, he was only a clerk. Knowing that the counter intelligence services could find out he was only a clerk, the suspect could appear to have made a confession about a relatively modest matter when, in reality, he had just followed a planned turn in his narrative.

No examination of interrogation techniques is complete without mentioning torture. There are three possible outcomes when using torture to extract specific information. The first is that if the subject actually knows nothing, he will make up information to bring the torture to a halt. If this happens, the interrogation team will waste valuable time in following false information. The second possible result is that the subject does know the truth but will offer apparently credible but false information as a distraction. A point made in histories about resisting interrogation is that being able to hold out for a certain amount of time will enable the subject's partners to escape. The third and most desirable outcome is that the subject knows the truth and will give that information to the interrogators. At the same time, the information must be vetted with valuable time spent evaluating it.

Historians of World War II generally acknowledge that torture was widely used by both the Allies and the Germans. When the survival of Britain was at stake, there is little doubt that the senior leadership— including Prime Minister Churchill—did not let moral and ethical considerations stand in the way of extracting intelligence. Essential to the success of the D-Day landings was the work of the Double Cross committee. This body was responsible for taking German agents who had been captured in the UK and convincing them to send broadcasts to Berlin that were written for them by the British command. The captured agents were told that if they could be turned, their war years would be completed in relative comfort. If they chose not to accept the British offer, they would be executed. Between those extreme options, selected torture would be used in convincing the Germans to work for the Allies.

The reason this deception plan, known as Operation Fortitude, worked is that all of the Abwehr agents in England had been turned. They sent back information suggesting that the D-Day invasion would take place at Calais rather than Normandy so the German forces remained at Calais believing the military operations at Normandy were a feint. Because of Britain's rigid security training, first-hand accounts of their torture did not appear and for decades there were not even indirect disclosures about things that happened. In terms of detecting a lie, Operation Fortitude is significant because it is not an individual that was targeted, but rather the German intelligence services. Therefore, what might be regarded as the interrogation process was indirect and depended on careful analysis of reports by German observers located in other countries. More importantly, the Germans had *no photo reconnaissance capabilities* in Scotland and could not accurately scrutinize reports about an Allied force set to invade Norway. There was no opportunity for someone like Colonel Alexis von Roenne, who had great influence on Hitler, to conduct an interrogation of Allied agents. Von Roenne headed the branch of German intelligence that evaluated the strength of Allied forces. In his calculations of the strength of Allied forces in Britain, he erred on the side of caution and greatly overestimated the number of Allied forces available for D-Day. In so doing, he gave the impression that the Allies had enough men and equipment in Britain to attack both Calais and Normandy.

In the year before D-Day, the Allies mounted another deception operation which was also helped by the participation of Colonel von Roenne. This was an especially complex endeavor known as Operation Mincemeat. The objective of Mincemeat was to convince the Germans that Allied planning called for an invasion of Greece and Sardinia rather than having 160,000 of their troops invade Sicily in July. The success of the operation was quickly seen as the German command directed that measures to be taken in Sardinia and the Peloponnese took priority over all others. A panzer division was transferred from France to Sardinia in anticipation of an Allied attack that never came.

The entire Mincemeat case demonstrates the complexity of the detection of lies and deceptions in a national security case. It is consistent with the observation of Columbia University political scientist

Richard Betts that there is an inverse relationship between accuracy and significance when evaluating national security information. First, a principle figure in this operation, William Martin, could not be interrogated because he was dead. What would have constituted the first step in a normal interrogation was not possible. Moreover, the architects of this operation, Ewen Montagu and Charles Cholmondeley, were both unknown and unavailable. Another figure, Dudley Clarke, who was responsible for deception operations in the Mediterranean, was even more obscure. These crucial figures were a blank in the calculations of the Germans who needed to determine the legitimacy of the elements of Mincemeat.

The basic idea of this innovative plot was that the body of a British courier would wash up on the beach of a specific Spanish village. A briefcase containing sensitive documents about Allied invasion plans would be chained to the body. An important stage of the operation was creating and collecting the pocket litter that would be in the pockets of Major William Martin's uniform. This included ticket stubs to prove the man actually had a life, letters from a bank telling him his account was in arrears, a bill from his tailor, and even a note from his girlfriend. His shoes needed to show an appropriate amount of wear as did his uniform itself. Because the British assumed his corpse would be subjected to an autopsy, they were careful to insure that his lungs would be sufficiently waterlogged. While there were ways to check on some of these specifics, the Germans needed to be discrete lest the British assume their ploy had been rejected. While the Germans might detect this as a hoax, it was better that the British not realize that the Germans saw it as a hoax.

The next stage to be carefully planned was after Martin's body washed up on the Spanish coast and was subjected to an autopsy. It was vital that the forged documents he carried actually be read by the Germans but, at the same time, it was essential that the Germans have a hard time getting their hands on them. After a strategic delay, the British set out to make it appear that they were desperate to get Martin's briefcase. Their search had to be diligent but not so diligent that it prevented the Germans from reading the documents. If the

British made the German effort too easy, there would have been a suspicion that the Martin information was planted. A crucial consideration was that the Germans saw the documents but believed that the British did not know they had read the documents. After all, if the British knew the Germans read the documents, they could simply change their invasion plans. Therefore, the operation would work only if the Germans were fooled into believing that the British had been fooled into believing the Spanish returned the briefcase unopened.

The commander of all German forces in the Mediterranean, Field Marshal Albert Kesselring, believed Sicily was the likely target, as did Benito Mussolini. Many of the senior officers in the German Navy and Air Force believed Sardinia was the target. Hitler and the German armed-forces High Command expected the attack to be in Greece. All of these conclusions were little more than *strategic inferences* based on an analysis of certain facts. As such, they were vague and imprecise. The material in Major William Martin's briefcase, however, was specific and thus had a major impact on German thinking. The decisive factor was how the Martin documents arrived. Intelligence professionals were suspicious of anything that was, in effect, given to them. What made the information more compelling was the apparent difficulty the Germans felt they faced in trying to get access to the briefcase. These strategic inferences were a substitute for the sort of interrogation associated with a less complex case.

Equally perplexing is the circuitous path by which this information made its way from a Spanish village to Berlin. The principal mover was Major Karl-Erich Kühlenthal who was the head of German intelligence in Spain. Kühlenthal was ambitious and his promotion of these materials was apparently driven by his belief that taking them directly to Berlin would enhance his career. In his messages to Berlin, Kühlenthal consistently embellished his assessments to the point where they seemed almost fictional. It was not so much that he believed in their authenticity but that he *needed* them to be authentic. Alexis von Roenne also indicated his support for the Martin documents but there is speculation he vouched for them because he doubted their veracity. His hatred for Hitler motivated him because he felt accepting Mincemeat would guarantee a defeat for Hitler. In the world of intelligence, secrets are confined to a small group of people, most of whom have a private agenda. This kind of information is proprietary and is not the product of careful institutional analysis. Each of the key individuals associated with an analysis of the documents had his own particular self-interest, none of which was necessarily consistent with Hitler's interest.

The Germans were prevented from undertaking a thorough analysis of all of the Mincemeat factors. In order to take advantage of the Martin documents, they needed to prevent the British from finding out that they knew about them. As the Germans saw it, if the British knew the Germans had access to this information, they would simply change their plans, making the information useless. Therefore, the Germans had to maintain an outwardly casual attitude about what was contained in Martin's briefcase. Had they conducted a thorough interview of the coroner, they might have seen the imperfections in the condition of the body. It might have been apparent that the body had deteriorated more than what would have been expected in the five day period indicated by the documents. Of course, further research about Mincemeat indicates that Ewen Montagu and Charles Cholmondeley might have been able to secure the body of a sailor whose death was more recent. This would explain the apparent detour that they took as they prepared to set out to sea with the body of Major Martin.

The final point about the impact of Operation Mincemeat is that it depended on the Germans being fooled into thinking the British had been deceived. The scheme was dependent on a multitude of events, any one of which might not have worked out as the British hoped. Professor Harold L. Wilensky, who was a specialist on organizational intelligence, observed that the higher the level of secrecy, the fewer intelligence people had access to the information. At the same time, the distribution of information would be less systematic. With the case of the Martin documents, there was uncertainty about authorship of the materials as well as an increasing intolerance regarding dissenting opinions. Wilensky believed that healthy arguments about an intelligence product were essential to the intelligence process and eventual product. Because of the restrictions inherent in the deliberations about Operation Mincemeat, the prospects for detection of deception were made more difficult. Even when it is relatively easy to check specific facts on the ground, interpretations of an adversary's intentions will remain inherently ambiguous.

The watchword for such a deception operation is expressed in the statement "They know you know they know you know." The complexity of this proposition indicates the difficulty of conducting any sort of examination of the facts of the case. With Operation Mincemeat there was no opportunity at all for any relevant interrogation and the responsible officials were limited to conjecture and supposition about motives. As a result, the entire crew—Hitler, Kühlenthal, and von Roenne made their decision based on guesses, which were incorrect. Shortly before the invasion, a British officer accidently left a classified document that outlined facts of the operation on a table in a hotel in Cairo. Instead of being devastating to Mincemeat, this mistake ended up strengthening the operation. The Germans were sure that something that had so easily fallen into their hands must have been a plant. In the end, it added strength to the German assumption that the attack would be against Greece and Sardinia. The decisive moment for the British came in a message from Bletchley Park which reported the German cables indicated the Germans had accepted the premise of Operation Mincemeat.

In a similar fashion, when the British discovered that a French officer in Algiers was actually a spy for the Germans, they kept him in place but fed him misleading information. When they realized the Germans feared he was actually a double agent, they allowed him to report that the D-Day invasion would be in Normandy. It was their correct expectation that such a report from the French officer would be the final piece of evidence that Normandy was not the invasion site.

While it appears that the Germans were totally dependent on assumption and conjecture, according to the published account of Operation Mincemeat—*The Man Who Never Was*—they did exercise several traditional methods of detecting deceptions. Allegedly, an Irish spy was sent to London to determine the verifiable facts.

First, he visited the facility where Martin had supposedly lived and confirmed that someone by that name had stayed there. Next, he visited the bank which had sent a letter to Martin warning about an overdraft. Pretending to be a friend, the Irish spy went to the bank to pay the money Martin owed. Third, he determined that the girlfriend who allegedly wrote letters to Martin was a real person. These confirmations were logical matters that the Germans could discreetly investigate. (Of course, it may well be that the account of an Irish spy checking on Martin was simply a dramatic embellishment to improve the story when it became a movie.)

The larger question relates to a strategic deception and the apparent motives reflected in the elements of the William Martin saga. The documents in his possession did carry the actual signatures of the supposed authors of those documents. The Germans had copies of their authentic signatures that could be studied to determine the veracity of the signatures on the letters in the briefcase. But, in the final analysis, the important question of where the Allied attack would be was left up to people trying to make a logical guess. If an analysis contains too many so-called "weasel words"—"perhaps," "likely," or "possibly"—the analysis will carry less weight.

Investigating a strategic deception operation is more difficult than investigating a spy case. The magnitude of such an undertaking defies many professional investigative techniques. By contrast, the effort to catch a Soviet/Russian spy in the CIA—Aldrich Ames—could be approached very differently. The long effort to identify this spy reflected more conventional methods of counter intelligence. A case such as this has more in common with the interrogation techniques used for criminal investigations.

Investigatory Techniques and Deceptions

IN A CRIMINAL INVESTIGATION THERE IS considerable dependence on information provided by people. To collect this human-source information, police generally begin with interviews of victims, witnesses or possible suspects. These interviews are usually non-accusatory and are inquiries about what someone heard or saw. The subject of the interview is expected to do most of the talking while the investigator simply asks questions and keep detailed records. When examining those records, if he spots a lie, he will confront the witness later. There may be times when an interview will become an interrogation if the subject is caught in an egregious lie.

One specific type of an interview is known as a cognitive interview. The objective of the cognitive interview is to reconstruct all the details of an incident. Subjects are encouraged to speak slowly and carefully. In order to facilitate this, there should be no tension or accusations. A witness will be encouraged to think about the circumstances of the incident, including things like the weather or the condition of the place of the incident. The goal is to accumulate all of the impressions of the witness even if they do not seem especially relevant. At the end of a cognitive interview, investigators should have a complete picture of what happened and the order of specific elements of the event.

It is important to distinguish between an interview and an interrogation. There is sometimes a tendency outside the law enforcement community to avoid the word interrogation because it has negative connotations. However, the terms interview and interrogation are not interchangeable because their purposes are different. The interview is non-custodial and the person being interviewed can leave at any time.

The interview will often seem like a casual conversation in which first names are used while the subject and the questioner appear to be on the same authority level. The investigator often tries to minimize the significance of the crime at this stage.

The time for confrontations will generally be during the interrogation process. During an interrogation, the investigators will direct their accusations, if warranted, against the subject who has now become a suspect. This is an extremely important part of any investigation and the term interrogation reflects a specific goal of the person directing this process. If the investigator uses misrepresentations at any point, this can undermine the entire process, especially if the suspect realizes this is happening.

There are several specific deceptions that may be used to gain information from a suspect. One is to tell the person that he is free to leave at any time. This makes the interview non-custodial and eliminates safeguards designed to protect the accused. For example, there will be no need for a Miranda warning under these circumstances. Another method of deception is to exaggerate the seriousness of the offense being investigated. This tactic is known as maximization. This will tend to frighten the suspect and make him speak more than is advisable. You might also use minimization as a tactic to understate the significance of the offense and thus encourage the suspect to speak more freely and casually. The investigator can make vague promises about the good things that will happen if there is a confession. Sometimes an investigator will actually deny that he is an investigator and pass himself off as an advocate for the suspect. If the suspect refuses to give a DNA sample the police can secure a sample anyway by offering a soft drink or a cup of coffee to the person being interrogated. Afterwards, they carefully use the cup or the can so they can get a DNA sample off the rim. A final example of deception techniques is demonstrated when an interrogator appears to give the suspect an advantage. He might say that he will turn off the recording so the suspect can speak off the record in a more candid fashion. The trick here is that the recording has not actually stopped so the suspect continues to speak not realizing he is incriminating himself.

The manner in which the investigator speaks can also constitute deception. Being overly casual helps convince the suspect that he is not really in trouble. Thus, he lets his guard down and responds to questions without thinking. He may also talk about "clearing up a misunderstanding" as a way of disarming an otherwise apprehensive subject or simply correcting a problem. These statements imply that everything might be "worked out" informally without anyone being in legal jeopardy.

These tactics may be deceptive but are not illegal. Of course, just because they are legal does not make them ethical. Ethical behavior is a requirement if the system is to enjoy the respect of those who depend on it to resolve inappropriate behavior that could undermine the efficacy of the system.

Having interactions with the suspect outside the interrogation site is another deceptive tactic. It is a way to get the suspect to provide information because he thinks he is being interviewed for a criminal job. When dealing with the most recalcitrant suspects, Canadian law enforcement officials utilize a time consuming procedure that involves having an undercover officer visit places where the uncooperative suspect goes for relaxation. By casually meeting the suspect, the undercover officer asks him if he is interested in working with the group of which he is a part. There will be a hint that the work is probably illegal but not dangerous. Eventually the tasks become more demanding and involve things such as stealing cars. As the relationship develops, the undercover policeman encourages the suspect to discuss his criminal CV in non-specific ways. After a few months, the suspect will be introduced to the "boss" of the gang, who is another undercover officer. This proceeds much like a job interview in which the "boss" demands details of the suspect's criminal past before he can include him as a regular part of his organization. Because he really needs this work, the suspect will have to share specific details of his criminal activities and will share information about the crime that the police had been investigating. When he provides those details, he is promptly arrested and the police can charge him on the basis of information he freely gave to the undercover officers.

Specialists recognize the distinction between interviews and interrogations. The subject of an investigation, assuming he has not had the benefit of training, is less aware of this distinction. In the UK and New Zealand, police officers often use a tactic designed to blur the distinction between the two. They begin in a friendly manner to make the encounter seem like a casual interview. Questioning proceeds very slowly and in an indirect fashion so the subject will not realize he is actually a suspect. This approach contains a subtle element of coercion but the suspect should not even realize what is happening until it is too late. This can often be effective in securing a confession but it is a lengthy process and requires both patience and time.

Interrogation Techniques
for Criminal Investigations

FOR MANY YEARS, POLICE INTERROGATIONS RELIED on various forms of torture. Until the early 20th century, physical abuse was widely practiced and even accepted in courts. By the 1960s, police interrogation techniques were reformed and courts would not accept a confession obtained by torture. Eventually, a confession was seen as forced if the suspect had been deprived of food, water, sleep, or bathroom facilities. With the Miranda ruling in 1966, police were required to inform a suspect that he had the right to remain silent and that an attorney would be provided to represent him.

When police were deprived of traditional ways of extorting a confession, they turned to a variety of psychological techniques. One of the most common was known as the "good cop/bad cop" routine. When this was used, police often found that a suspect would confide in the police officer who seemed sympathetic while avoiding the abusive partner. As noted earlier, another psychological technique was called maximization. This involved scaring a suspect by telling him all of the terrible things that would happen to him in court—and in prison—if he did not cooperate. Police also tried to intimidate suspects by subjecting them to a polygraph examination. This was not very useful because polygraph training was so expensive and bringing in a contractor was also an unwieldy procedure. Even if the polygraph produced useful results, they were generally inadmissible in court. In connection with the polygraph, a man named John E. Reid developed an interrogation system that was not based on a machine but rather on the application of questions that would normally produce physical reactions similar to those detectable by the polygraph. Reid's "Nine Steps" of psychological manipulation were eventually adopted by many police departments across the United States.

Another advantage that police enjoy is that they can lie to suspects, a common and legal phenomenon. There is a casual assumption that a suspect would never confess if he were not guilty. Unfortunately, a frightened, vulnerable person can easily be tricked into confessing if he believes the police actually have evidence proving his guilt or are willing to let him go home once he confesses. A hopeless suspect will feel that the odds are stacked against him from the outset. This sort of deception is a part of psychological manipulation that has been accepted in courts across the country.

Under the worst of circumstances this sort of pressure can actually manufacture fake memories that might trigger a false confession. According to a German study that was reported in 2021, scientists have been able to convince patients that they had traumatic childhood experiences. This might include being in automobile accidents or getting lost in a forest. At the same time, the study examined ways in which interrogators might be able to determine if a person is acting on the basis of manufactured memories and how those memories might be eliminated.

It is vital that interrogators undermine the confidence of their suspect. If the suspect tries to specifically deny their accusations, the interrogators will not allow him to complete a denial statement. Allowing a suspect to speak may convince him that he has the ability to mount a self-defense. If he is allowed to elaborate a defense, he will be attentive to the expressions of the police and will look for a glimmer of acceptance. The prisoner must always be manipulated and believe his situation is hopeless. This can be accomplished if the interrogator seems calm and understanding. An effective interrogator may imply that he is sympathetic to the suspect and that he understands how he feels. Some people compare a skillful interrogator to a priest who has empathy. In this way, the police can minimize the crime that is being investigated. Sensing that the interrogator wants to help will make it easier for the suspect to confess. If an interrogator is revolted by the suspect, he must not show this. On the other hand, if he is actually sympathetic to and likes the suspect, he must also hide this. The key point is that after a long period of sensory deprivation or solitary confinement, a suspect is more vulnerable and more inclined to open up to an apparently sympathetic questioner. He may have a desire to talk after his long isolation so someone must be with him and ready to listen.

Many criminals feel a need for recognition of their work and take pride in their actions. This can be exploited by allowing a suspect to correct what he may see as an investigator's misperceptions of what he has done. If he is motivated by a political cause, he will welcome the chance to speak to an essentially captive audience. If the person feels shame for his misdeeds, the interrogator can explain ways in which he can atone for them. In the case of murderers who have hidden the bodies of their victims, they can help by leading police to the graves of their victims. Police will tell them that they will be more favorably remembered if they help the victims' families provide a proper burial for loved ones. If the suspect is part of a criminal organization and fears reprisals for helping the police, he can be shown ways in which he will be protected, such as through the Witness Security Program.

Even if he is not guilty, the suspect will be attracted by the idea of confessing to a crime of lesser magnitude. The suspect may hope that if he is cooperative, he may be treated better in court. As long as the suspect feels there is no reasonable way he can prove his innocence, he will be looking for a better way out. At a minimum, he will want to try to shape the narrative in such a way that he does not look so bad. If the police refer to his crime as a "mistake" rather than something more severe, it will make him more likely to confess. If he can do this without seeming to be the bad guy in a complicated case, it is a more attractive option.

Before beginning the real interrogation, there should be a preliminary interview. The purpose of this event is to determine if the suspect could possibly be the person who committed the crime. It might become apparent within the first few minutes that he is not a credible suspect, and so the police don't waste their time. The initial interview gives the interrogators an opportunity to establish rapport with their subject. This can be accomplished by discussing routine matters such as an interest in sports teams. When the subject starts talking about non-threatening issues he will relax. With this atmosphere, it is harder for him to stop talking when the topic changes.

This conversation will help establish a baseline about the interviewee's reactions to different subjects. There will be specific eye movements associated with each mental process, for example. When the interrogator has identified a baseline for non-threatening subjects, he can more accurately assess times in which the subject's reactions change. The starting point would be to ask simple questions that require memory and note any actions, such as eye movement, that are associated with remembering a fact. From these questions, move to ones that require the subject to think in solving a mental puzzle. This requires creativity and stimulates a part of the brain that is different from simple recall. There will be a movement of the eyes associated with activation of the cognitive center of the brain. By noting eye activity, the interrogator will further develop a baseline for the suspect's responses to particular types of questions.

These questions in the initial interview prepare for the more direct questions about the crime. If asked where he was on the night of the crime, an honest suspect will simply have to remember where he was. A dishonest suspect will have to invent an alibi and this will require creativity and an eye movement. As the detective studies the suspect's eye movements he may be able to determine if he is being deceptive.

If the interrogator believes the suspect is deceptive, he will move to a part of the interrogation process that involves confrontation. This begins with a presentation of the evidence—both real and false— against the suspect. When the police officer says "we know you are guilty," there should be a significant increase in the suspect's stress level. This process can be accelerated if the interrogator invades the personal space of the suspect. If the suspect is guilty, he is likely to fidget and use self-comforting grooming gestures, further indications of deception. On the other hand, if the interrogator has failed to gather all of the facts of the case, the suspect might recognize that shortcoming. When a suspect believes the interrogator is lying, he is less likely to accept any reassuring words or promises the interrogator makes. The interrogator can lie, but he must lie effectively if he is to enjoy an advantage during the interrogation process.

When he realizes the suspect is likely guilty, the interrogator can create a narrative that will explain why the suspect committed the crime. A non-threatening approach will make it easier for the suspect to accept the narrative, especially if some element of the narrative seems to excuse his actions. This might be a suggestion that the victim had provoked him so his response was understandable. If the suspect appears to listen more carefully at this point that will indicate his acceptance of the story the interrogator has developed. As noted elsewhere, it is important to prevent the suspect from making any denials that would build confidence in his ability to defend himself. The interrogator should tell the suspect he needs to listen at this time but will have time when he can talk later. If the suspect remains silent, he will not be able to ask for an attorney. If the suspect does not offer any sort of denial, this will be viewed as another indication of guilt.

It is possible at this point that the suspect will not make explicit denials but will offer an objection based on logic. He might say that he would never do such a thing because a member of his family had been a victim of such a crime. If the interrogator responds to that by saying "I understand your feelings and realize this may have been an accident, that you intended no harm," in this manner, the interrogator is taking the suspect's statement as simply another indication of guilt or, at best, self-justification. As a result, the suspect's insecurity will increase and he will be looking for some sort of relief or support. By giving a reassuring gesture such as a pat on the back, the interrogator can appear sympathetic without saying anything that might be a withdrawal from his narrative of the suspect's guilt.

At this point, the suspect's body language may indicate that he has given up and will simply look for some justification of his actions. An effective interrogator will offer reasons for why the suspect might have committed the crime and put him in a position where he must select one of the offered options. Maintaining eye contact is a vital move at this time and will help the suspect finally confess to the crime. The interrogator will want to bring another detective into the room so the suspect can make his confession in front of a new person who has not led him to it. If the suspect can elaborate on his "socially acceptable" reasons for committing the crime, this will strengthen his resolve to make a formal confession that he can sign. By doing this, the suspect will conclude that his confession is final and be more ready to accept the consequences. In order to be sure that he has obtained a confession that will be accepted during the trial, the interrogator may have the suspect make a video statement of his confession and indicate that the confession was not coerced.

The physical layout of the interrogation room is something else that gives the police advantages. It is always best (for the police) if the interrogation takes place in a police facility. By operating from their own building, police can use a two way mirror so other police officers can watch the interrogation to determine which lines of inquiry seem most effective. It increases the discomfort of the suspect if he is not near light switches or thermostats. This makes him more dependent on the authorities to satisfy his requirements and underscores his helpless situation. If that is not possible and you are in the suspect's home, the key to a successful interrogation will be to arrange the room in such a way that the subject is less comfortable. One way to do this is to position the interrogator with the window behind him. Therefore, the subject finds himself staring into the light coming through the window, a situation that will make him uncomfortable. If police are conducting the interrogation in the suspect's home, it is important that he not feel it is his home. Move furniture around so the place looks and feels different. It will weaken the suspect's confidence if the police have taken control of his home. The suspect should be seated in an uncomfortable chair while the interrogator has a nice chair. Equally important is that the suspect realizes he cannot just walk out when he wants to because he is a "prisoner." This is not an "interview" and he will be there as long as the police want him to be.

Another important weapon is the police case file, which can contain all of the information about the suspect. The subject cannot be sure just how much the police know so he will suffer from a certain amount of uncertainty. As long as the interrogator has gathered all of the facts relating to the crime, he will enjoy an advantage. If the interrogation has been long—perhaps running for several days—it will be hard for him to remember exactly what he said previously. His confusion will become an important factor. It is relatively easy for the police—with their abundant resources—to find a contradiction in his statements. This could provide an opening for the next stage of the questioning.

Even if torture yields a positive result, it still leaves its practitioners with an important dilemma. The use of torture is a human rights violation. The utilization of torture can have a poisonous impact on society if it is successful because it will create a culture in which all values are sacrificed in the search for evidence. Moreover, while a sound beating has an overwhelming impact on a suspect, in the long run anxiety, humiliation, and loneliness are more powerful tools in breaking the subject of the interrogation.

One of the most notorious forms of torture in recent years has been a practice known as waterboarding. This is an old technique that can be traced back to the Spanish Inquisition but it became a controversy because of its use by American personnel during the so-called war on terror. During waterboarding, the subject is placed on an inclined board with his feet elevated. Water is poured over his face while a cloth face covering prevents the water from flowing away. This simulates drowning and is done repeatedly. It causes great psychological damage but leaves no physical marks.

During the Middle Ages, the main purpose of torture was punishment rather than information-gathering. The suspect was assumed to be guilty and was simply receiving punishment. This was not an effort to gather information. A person in pain is not going to be an accurate reporter, so the information he may provide is not likely to be accurate. While we are no longer in the Middle Ages, the Iranians routinely use torture as a bargaining tactic. When they arrested the Swedish disaster medicine specialist Ahmadreza Djalali, they endeavored to exchange him for Assadollah Assadi, a senior officer in Iran's intelligence service and a convicted terrorist serving a twenty year sentence in a Belgian prison. Ahmadreza Djalali, who had directed projects designed to help hospitals respond to terrorist attacks, was subjected to torture not because he had information to give but because the torture gave Swedish and Belgian officials a time line to follow. The death of Djalali would simply serve as revenge if Assadi was not freed.

During the Northern Ireland conflict in the 1970s, British troops were guilty of misusing many interrogation techniques. As a result of extensive investigations, the British government issued directives that specifically outlawed the use of hooding, wall standing, excessive noise, and the deprivation of sleep or food. In spite of these policy changes, there were violations by British personnel in Iraq in the 2000s.

American personnel have been involved in similar controversies regarding various forms of torture. Activities at Guantanamo Bay as well as other secret sites have generated criticism and calls for further reforms of interrogation procedures. During the war in Iraq, the Abu Ghraib prison was the scene of well publicized incidents of torture. Employees of the Central Intelligence Agency and US military personnel were involved in physical and sexual abuse of prisoners, rape, sodomy, and even murder. Other incidents were reported at Camp Nama, a secret facility located at Baghdad International Airport where members of the US military's Task Force 121 attempted to gather information about the location of Saddam Hussein. There is no ambivalence in US policies on torture, which is categorized as a war crime for which there is no statute of limitations. These policies are applicable to military, civilians, and defense contract personnel.

Not only is torture illegal, it is also widely considered to be immoral and unethical, and it has been denounced as a violation of the fundamental principles of human rights. Perhaps even more powerful arguments can be made against torture because it is clearly not reliable and does not produce intelligence of practical operational value. Moreover, contemporary conflicts feature extensive propaganda efforts and incidents such as those in Abu Ghraib can make enemy propaganda much more effective.

The most common interrogation technique in the United States was developed by a private company called John E. Reid and Associates, Inc. It began developing interview and interrogation techniques in 1947. Reid Associates runs training courses for interrogators and claims to have trained more interrogators than any other company in the world. The Reid slogan is that they protect the innocent and identify the guilty. Reid founded a technique that is based on three components. These components are factual analysis, interviewing, and interrogation. Factual analysis is an effort to look at each possible suspect in terms of motivations and access to the crime scene. Another factor is the suspect's inclination to commit a particular crime. If the suspect is known as a sexual offender and the police are investigating a rape case, then that suspect is rated higher as a likely perpetrator. Physical evidence is taken into consideration along with the personality of the suspect as well as all the information that can be gathered about each suspect.

The second component involves interviews and is referred to as the Behavior Analysis Interview. The interview will start with background questions that will enable the interrogator to study a suspect's verbal *and nonverbal behavior*. The investigator will then ask questions that are designed to provoke certain types of behavior such as anger, fear, or hostility. The investigator will make certain assumptions about the suspect based on these reactions. During the course of the behavior analysis interview which is non-confrontational, the investigator should be able to establish rapport with the suspect. This is important in setting a baseline for later reactions during more confrontational questioning. It will also help in the development of an overall interrogation strategy.

The final component is interrogation. Contrasted with the interview phase, the interrogation should not begin until the investigator is reasonably certain that the suspect has some involvement with the crime in question. The first step in interrogation is a positive confrontation in which the interviewer tells the suspect that he knows he is guilty. If the interviewer feels certain about this, he should make the positive confrontation more emphatic. The next step involves the development of a theme that might facilitate a confession. For example, the interviewer might observe that the victim's behavior was a contributing factor that could justify an assault. At this stage, the suspect should be discouraged from speaking because the interrogator doesn't want him to deny the accusation. If the suspect manages to say that he would never have done whatever the crime may have been, the investigator should accept that denial without comment. It is important to keep the suspect's attention focused on the theme being developed by the interviewer. Meanwhile, the interviewer should maintain a sympathetic demeanor and continue to stress psychological justifications for the crime. If he is successful in giving the suspect two choices as an explanation for the crime, it is likely that the suspect will select the choice which puts him in a better light. If one option allows a confession based on something that was unintentional, the suspect is more likely to embrace this one. Once he has done this, the investigator should ask the suspect to make a brief oral statement in order to avoid "confusion." When the confession has been stated orally, it will be necessary to have a written or recorded confession.

As should be expected, there are criticisms of the Reid Technique. The most common objection to this approach is that it is based on an assumption that the suspect is guilty. The guilt-presumptive nature of the program is said to produce false confessions. Critics argue that the Reid program incorrectly identifies honest people as dishonest, that suspects are subjected to psychological manipulation, and that police contaminate confessions by providing suspects with non-public information that works its way into the confession. While the Reid program instructors maintain that they can train investigators to distinguish between honest denials and dishonest denials, critics argue that, in general, people are simply not very good in making good judgments about when people are being truthful or deceptive.

As an alternative to Reid's excessively confrontational approach, in Britain there is widespread usage of a different technique. The British method is known as Preparation and Planning, Engage and Explain, Account, Closure and Evaluate or by the acronym PEACE. Under the British system, suspects can tell their story and investigators will not interrupt them. The interrogator is not allowed to lie to suspects and he must save his response to the suspect's statement until the suspect has finished. The interrogator should prepare a written plan for the interview before starting the process. There is a national body of guidance on policing that spells out requirements of this system. It is known as the Authorized Professional Practice (APP). The objective of APP is to coordinate the work of all of the UK police organizations in such a way as to implement reforms and generate evidence-based knowledge.

The APP was established by the UK College of Policing, which employees six hundred staff members who work as trainers, coaches, assessors, designers, and expert witnesses. Recognizing that police encounters are often traumatic, the APP includes specific guidance on the circumstances under which people may be stopped and searched. For the British, the guidance is very simple. A legitimate stop and search must be fair, legal, professional in every aspect, and transparent. The police powers of stop and search must always meet these four requirements.

There are also explicit requirements about all interactions between the police and those people whom they interview. The first concern is that police must explain why they have stopped a person and they must also explain routines they will use throughout the conversation. The individual should be encouraged to talk and the officers must work to establish rapport with the interviewees. This means they must employ the techniques of active listening at all times while ensuring that notes are taken. Questions should be short and to the point and officers should avoid multi-part questions that might lead to confusion. Finally, rather than ending the interview abruptly, officers should close with a summary of what has been revealed and give the suspect the opportunity to offer corrections or ask questions. As the process ends, the police officers who participated in it should take time to determine how the suspect's account fits with the case as they understand it. This is also the time to decide what further actions need to be taken, who else might be interviewed, or if they need to bring the suspect back for further questions at a later time.

Closely related to this approach is the *kinesic* interview technique, which appeared in 1952. This technique was developed by the American anthropologist Ray Birdwhistell who wrote several books on culturally-based patterns of visual communication. For him, the term *kinesic* referred to facial expression, gestures, posture and gait, and visible arm and body movements. It was derived from the Greek term for movement. *Kenesic*, therefore, replaced the older term "non-verbal communications." Initially, *kenesic* techniques were used in the studies of anthropology and linguistics but they eventually gained acceptance as an interview technique. In a broad sense, *kinesics* is a complex structure of body movements which are, in effect, a formalized language code. The motions a person makes in response to questions can be effective in determining if he is honest. According to Birdwhistell, during most conversations, 70% of the information is obtained by observing nonverbal signals such as facial expressions.

The objective of the *kinesic* interview method is to analyze the behavior of the suspect for indications of deception. There are two phases in the process. The first is the analysis phase, during which the interviewer will utilize the techniques most likely to determine the balance between the subject's truthful and deceptive behaviors. When this is accomplished, he can identify sensitive areas that can be probed by a further questioning. The second phase is the interrogation phase during which the interviewer will use the information gathered during the analysis phase to shape the themes for interrogation. The analysis phase will establish the personality type of the subject and enables the interviewer to determine the level of aggression to be employed. During interrogation, the interviewer will confront the suspect's emotional state as a way of directing him toward an eventual confession.

For a person using the *kinesic* interview technique, the goal is to be able to determine the relationship between the subject's words and actions. From the first, the interviewer will notice the subject's behavior in terms of comfort levels and gestures. As the questioning goes to issues more directly related to a crime, it will be important to observe changes in nonverbal behaviors. The challenge for the interviewer is to make note of when the nonverbal behavior is altered and determine which questions have sparked the changes. This will point him toward those areas of deception. Specific physical indicators could be evidence of a dry mouth, changes in breathing patterns, self-comforting gestures such as smoothing of the hair, or suddenly not making eye contact.

The *kinesic* method is typically non-aggressive and based on the assumption that most subjects will respond better to this approach. This will change when dealing with a person who refuses to cooperate or is hostile. In this case, a more aggressive method should be used. This is referred to as a *tactical kinesic* technique. If a certain type of question has caused the suspect to change his body language, the interviewer will want to follow that theme. A question about a suspicious activity will not likely affect an innocent person but the guilty suspect will become more uncomfortable. The question which elicits that response is known as a *kinesic* question and should drive the investigatory narrative.

Practical Interrogation Guidance

THERE ARE SOME BASIC ASSUMPTIONS ABOUT how an investigator should conduct the interrogation process. These are generally applicable within the context of most styles of interrogations. In an important sense, they can be viewed as common sense on how to interact with people who find themselves in a subordinate position. The key point for the interrogator is that while he is in a dominant position, he should not adopt an offensive attitude of superiority.

As the interrogator enters the room, he should assume a relaxed attitude and show sympathy for the person who is in a difficult situation. He generally will not have to show the suspect that he is the boss because the position of authority is assumed. The investigator will want to instill trust rather than to inspire fear. By being organized and confident, he will demonstrate that he is in control and have no need to act as a bully. Even if the suspect is difficult or irritating, it is essential that the interrogator remain calm. If a suspect is able to make his questioner angry, he has assumed control over the situation.

As can be seen from examples of successful interrogations, it is important that the interrogator establish a good relationship with the suspect. This can be accomplished by being polite, kind, and attentive to their needs. The interrogator's bar is fairly low at this point, and if he does something as basic as asking the suspect what he wants to be called, he will be seen as a reasonable person. Saying his first name frequently underscores this positive impression. A relaxed atmosphere during the early stages of an interrogation is enhanced by asking about the suspect's interests, discussing non-contentious topics like sports, and inquiring about the suspect's family background.

When beginning the interrogation, it is helpful to identify a basic need the suspect might have regarding something unrelated to the investigation. It might be something as simple as helping his family secure a government benefit like food stamps. If an investigator can make a call on behalf of the suspect, it creates an impression that the investigator is a fair person just trying to do his job. It is possible that the suspect's unrelated need is more important to him than the information the investigator needs for the investigation.

Another effective but indirect approach is to ask the suspect's opinions. First, this demonstrates that the investigator sees him as a person whose opinion is worth seeking. Second, if the investigator asks the suspect what he thinks should happen to a person who committed the crime being investigated, he may offer something that is helpful. If he says the perpetrator should go to prison, that shows what he is thinking and acknowledges that it is a serious concern. On the other hand, if he believes the person who committed the crime should pay a fine or lose his job, you know he is concerned on a different level. How he responds will betray his general assumptions about the crime.

While few suspects will be so naïve or unrealistic as to expect you to open the door for them, it is helpful if an interrogator can offer contrasting visions of what may happen to them. An interrogator can speak in terms of finding the best outcome rather than threatening the suspect with terrible punishments. If he is shown what may be considered as the best of several bad alternatives, the questioner can present himself as an advocate. He needs to resolve the case to satisfy his boss but he would like to get the suspect a more favorable outcome. This might be a matter of a five-year sentence as opposed to ten years in prison.

The proper phrasing of questions can create a productive interview. There should be a balance between open questions and closed questions. Closed questions are like those seen on a multiple choice test. The answer is either "yes," "no" or something specific like an address. Open questions require the suspect to talk. He may need to explain something or provide details about his alibi. If his response is long, he is more likely to slip up and give more information than he intended.

Another type of inquiry is known as a funnel question. If the suspect becomes comfortable talking to the investigator, he may begin to tell more of his story. The starting point is to ask something general about which you already have some knowledge. You might ask what people were in the office at a certain time. As he begins to name all of the people he may offer a clue about what happened.

An important objective is to get the suspect to speak freely. The "funnel question" can accomplish this and descriptive questions serve the same objective. By asking the suspect to describe a scene or to offer details of what he witnessed, he will begin to feel more comfortable with the sound of his own voice. And there are some suspects that really love the sound of their own voice and enjoy having an audience for their recollections. The monologue can reveal important information that could lead to a confession, or at least to the identification of other suspects.

Analytical questions, like most open ended queries, encourage a suspect to think more generally about a crime. If investigators ask him what type of person might have committed the crime being investigated, they can get an idea of how he thinks about people who might steal from an employee or who would do something to harm a child. This is one of those times when a careful observation of the suspect's body language would be helpful.

In asking questions it is important not to phrase them in a way that encourages certain types of responses. You might ask the suspect if he saw *the* man carrying a bucket. By saying "the man" rather than "a man," you have indicated that there was a certain man who was there. Accordingly, the suspect will be inclined to agree because the investigator suggested that such a man was there. On the other hand, if a suspect sees a question as being directed against him, he may become defensive and refuse to talk. Either way, such a leading question can push an investigation in the wrong direction and delay a resolution of the case. Another interrogation tactic is the so-called loaded question. This is a question that is based on an assumption that the suspect is guilty. An interrogator might ask "where did you go after leaving the bank?" This constitutes an accusation. If the suspect is actually innocent of robbing the bank, this line of questioning could disrupt the investigation effort. An interrogator might employ a dichotomous question that requires the suspect to answer "yes" or "no" rather than giving a detailed but more accurate response. After all, the correct answer might be "I don't know."

There are other effective tactics that can be used in dealing with a suspect. When the suspect responds to a question with an answer that seems untrue, the interrogator can respond with silence and a stare. Most people in Western culture are uncomfortable with such silences and often feel a need to continue to talk just to fill the silence or break the stare.

The use of a prop may be effective. It is one of the ways an interrogator can suggest without speaking that he already has the information that might convict the suspect. If he enters the room with a file bulging with documents or photo negatives, the suspect will be uncomfortable even if nothing is said about these props. He will imagine that they might constitute some proof that he is guilty. On the other hand, if he is not guilty he will simply be puzzled and perhaps wonder if the interrogator has somewhere he must go immediately after this session.

Finally, there are certain basic traits that the interrogator must possess. The first essential characteristic is empathy. The interrogator should be able to identify with the subject in a sincere manner. If he shows he can view a situation through the eyes of the suspect, it makes it easier to secure a confession. A skillful interviewer should be able to create an environment in which two humans are communicating.

A second necessary characteristic is that the interrogator should be an effective communicator. Communication is more than just a word. It also includes the interviewer's tone of voice, his inflection, and his volume. The way in which he pauses can have a big impact on the subject of the interview as the pauses help him convey a helpful image to the suspect. Gestures, hand movements, or nodding of the head are part of the non-verbal communications of the interrogation.

A final helpful characteristic is professionalism. This includes how the interviewer dresses. There is a certain dress code when interviewing a factory worker, for example. If he interviews the CEO of a corporation he will dress more formally. The interview should begin with a handshake and end the same way. Another component of professionalism is the avoidance of snide remarks and the careful collection of all relevant details.

Interrogation and Investigation Failures

WITH ALMOST ANY SYSTEM THERE IS a realistic prospect of failure. That failure can take a variety of forms. For the Germans in World War II, dramatic failures occurred with the British invasion of Sicily and even more overwhelming on D-Day. These are historic failures. On a more individual level, there are countless investigative failures that have translated into innocent people being punished for crimes they did not commit.

The most immediate consequence of such a failure is that an innocent person goes to prison but it also ensures that the guilty party remains unpunished. In some cases, it is not simply a matter of an innocent person going to prison but some people are executed. Most cases of wrongful convictions have involved crooked prosecutors, unprepared or overworked defense attorneys, procedural errors, erroneous interrogations, and technology issues. Many people charged in such cases have often been poor or suffered from mental challenges, making it difficult for them to understand what was happening. Many falsely believed a confession meant that the interrogations would end and they could return home. Although it is sometimes difficult to prove, prejudice on the part of police sometimes could have been a factor. The advent of DNA testing and the increasing sophistication of those procedures have helped to reduce errors.

In addition to false confessions, wrongful convictions may occur because eyewitnesses have been mistaken in their identifications of suspects. This is most likely in the case of cross-racial identifications. Eyewitness testimony is notoriously inaccurate, but ineffective lawyers are another common factor in producing wrongful convictions. Many public defenders are routinely overworked, so they fail to check alibis or to challenge forensic evidence that is not properly done. Because police departments are so often understaffed, there is a great reliance on informants. Therefore, they don't realize when informants have some incentive to testify against a defendant. Informants can go into the business of informing in multiple cases in the hope of securing benefits such as reduced sentences or even bribes. Finally, while there is great popular faith in forensic science, many elements of this discipline are not based on sound principles. Many police departments place great faith in specializations such as bite mark analysis, shoe print comparisons, or microscopic hair comparisons without realizing that experts in these fields have a greater desire in cultivating their specializations and their careers. As a result, the claims they make are often not justified and the result is wrongful convictions. In the case of bite mark analysis, it is now roundly dismissed as "junk science."

One of the most notorious cases of a wrongful conviction is that of the so-called Central Park Five in 1989. When a young woman who had been jogging in Central Park was raped and severely beaten, police focused on five young men from Harlem who had also been in the park at the time. The victim was in a lengthy coma and when she awoke she had no memory of the attack and could provide no useful information. The five young men confessed but later claimed their confessions were coerced and that the police had intimidated them. Even though their statements were inconsistent with physical evidence, all five were convicted and received sentences ranging from five to thirteen years. In 2002, DNA testing in another case led police to a serial rapist who admitted that he had attacked the jogger and that he had been alone. On the basis of that confession, the sentences of the Central Park Five were vacated but they had already been released.

In 1997, another highly publicized case saw police essentially rejecting a confession to a rape and murder when that confession appeared to exonerate four young men who had been charged. When a woman in Norfolk, Virginia was murdered, police suspected her neighbors and subjected them to a lengthy, hostile interrogation. The two men were told they would be facing the death penalty unless they confessed.

Fearing the death penalty, they confessed and named two others as being involved in the crime. Eventually, all four confessed, even though one of the suspects, a sailor, had been deployed at sea when the crime took place. Moreover, all of their statements contradicted each other on important details. Years later, an incarcerated felon admitted that he had committed the crime without any other people being involved. His DNA was found at the crime scene. However, the Norfolk Four remained in prison because police insisted they had been accomplices of the person who confessed. By this time, one of the four had completed his sentence. Facing life sentences, the other three were given conditional pardons by Governor Tim Kaine.

The 1982 murder of 19-year-old Rebecca Lynn Williams in Virginia resulted in a death sentence for a farmhand who was in custody for a different crime. In 1983, after two full days of interrogation, police convinced an unfortunate Earl Washington Jr, who had an IQ of 69, to confess to five crimes. In his confession to the Williams murder, Washington got important details wrong. This included the site of the murder and the race of the murder victim. While four of Washington's confessions were thrown out, he was convicted for the Williams murder and sentenced to death. His execution was delayed when another prisoner filed a petition on his behalf and in 1994 the Governor commuted his death sentence to life in prison. In 2000, DNA testing proved Washington's innocence and he was freed. As is so often the case, while an unjustly convicted person languished in prison, the actual killer was never caught.

The examples cited above may have been well publicized but they are not atypical. Studies indicate that many prisoners now serving in American prisons were wrongfully convicted. Since 1989, the National Registry of Exonerations has reported that 2,645 people have been exonerated because of discovery of errors in their prosecutions. Each person has spent an average of almost nine years before finally being released following reversal of their convictions. Securing a reversal is a difficult challenge because the defendant must conclusively prove that his trial was unconstitutional because the police used coercion or failed to obtain a warrant. If he was wrongfully convicted because the factual evidence used by authorities was incorrect, the most common avenue for gaining a reversal is through the introduction of new DNA evidence.

There have been consistent efforts to reduce the dangerous phenomenon of the false confession. Regardless of the specific types of interrogation procedures that might be used, it is helpful to have an electronic recording of the entire process. For many years the norm was to have a "recorded confession." This is different from the electronic recording because it only included the confession itself and did not show an account of the process through which the confession was obtained. This procedure makes it easier to evaluate the confession and determine if it was in any way coerced.

Alternative Systems of Interrogation

THESE SYSTEMS WE'VE DISCUSSED REFLECT WESTERN values and ethical considerations but there are numerous others which are focused exclusively on promised results. This is the case even if the promised results never materialize. Systems that are illustrative of this are the Nazis during World War II, the Soviets and their allies over a longer period, and even the British during and after World War II. This list, of course, is not exhaustive, as there are other examples. Nor does the list invite comparisons in terms of the success each system enjoyed because their objectives were not all the same.

The Nazi regime has the worst reputation in terms of severe and brutal interrogation methods. They employed a variety of tactics including blackmail, extortion, sleep deprivation, and other inhumane methods of extracting confessions or information. Sometimes one of the most effective tactics was to do the unexpected. Former prisoner Corrie ten Boom recounted her surprise in meeting a new interrogator who was different from the previous thugs who had questioned her during her three months at an especially brutal camp. The new interrogator was polite and considerate of her comfort and welfare. However, because of her long experience with Nazi interrogators, she realized that his kind manner was simply a tactic intended to disarm her into giving information that would expose Dutch resistance fighters. When she realized he was trying to investigate ration card fraud, she knew she had nothing to tell him since she was not involved in this operation. His courteous and kind manner was all for nothing. Other Nazi interrogators would use this approach and take prisoners to a cabin in the woods where they would enjoy privileges. This was simply a sophisticated effort to establish rapport with prisoners in an effort to get them to betray their colleagues.

Hans Scharff was an effective Nazi interrogator who enjoyed success while also treating prisoners with courtesy and compassion. While he never resorted to torture, his suggestion that if they did not help him they might be turned over to the dreaded Gestapo was effective in getting information. Because he had previously worked in South Africa in his family's textile business he was proficient in English and his skills as a salesman were exceptional. Both of these attributes contributed to his success in interrogating downed Air Corps personnel. Prisoners always received generous food allotments and good medical care. Scharff wore civilian clothing and cultivated good relationships with the prisoners. Because of his cordial and effective manner, most prisoners did not realize they had given him any information of military value. Many prisoners wrote tributes to Scharff and after the war he was recruited by the Pentagon to work for the United States. He published a book about his experiences and eventually became a US citizen.

While there are exceptional instances of the employment of techniques that are disarming and unexpected, the Nazis were most often noted for their brutality. Some of the brutality was more psychological than physical and prisoners were subjected to physical hardships that would erode their ability to resist. The prisoner was continuously bombarded with questions and all of his answers would be rejected. This rejection set the stage for beginning the process all over again until the prisoner agreed to make the sort of confession required by the interrogators. Once imprisoned, the Nazis might turn up the heat in the prisoner's cell while he waited for the arrival of the interrogator. The objective was to intensify the prisoner's physical discomfort. With regard to physical methods used in interrogation, the Nazis were often cited for their monstrous inventiveness as they devised unique ways of torture. According to a report by the Supreme Allied Headquarters' Psychological Warfare Unit, other methods used by the Nazi security services included "putting people's hands in boiling water until the skin and fingernails came off like gloves; stomping on a man's foot for ten minutes with a special steel boot and repeating the process for two weeks; pressing a hot poker onto the hands; hanging people by their hands behind their backs until their shoulders were out of joint, then gashing the soles of their feet and making the victims walk on salt; pulling teeth and cutting and twisting off the ears; running electric current through the victims' bodies and using other fiendish devices." If these punishments were not enough to move a subject to confess, there was the ever-present threat to send the prisoner to one of the Nazi concentration camps, a move that would open up the possibility of even more tortures. Of course, these methods often resulted in the premature death of the subject. This was regarded as a failure if the prisoner had not provided the information being sought.

The methods used by Soviet Communists were in many ways similar to those used by Nazi security personnel. The levels of brutality varied in accordance with domestic conditions in particular regions. Lithuania and Ukraine had active guerilla movements in the early part of the 20th century, so investigations of those organizations were typically more brutal. There was a degree of variety in KGB interrogation methods but most commonly they began with psychological, rather than physical, torture. Upon being taken into the KGB headquarters building, before any words were exchanged, the prisoner would be stripped naked and placed in a small windowless closet for several hours. This gave the prisoner time to speculate about what he might have done to offend the authorities. It could be something relatively innocuous as telling an anti-Soviet joke or failing to meet a work quota. It was equally possible that he had been denounced by a neighbor or even a child. When taken to an interrogation room the questioning would begin with general matters such as "why are you an enemy of the people?" There would be demands for the names of co-conspirators. There might already be a confession prepared for them to sign. There were numerous twists and turns in a process that could take days, weeks, or even months. Some interrogations were known to last for days while others ran for years.

Soviet interrogators were instructed to always have a team to assist them in questioning a subject. This way there was always relief for their officers who needed to have periods of rest. The process would continue until there was a result. The first statement to the accused usually was to the effect that the authorities had irrefutable evidence of his guilt. An important part of the process was to give the subject paper so he could write a statement that had to begin with the declaration that he regretted his actions even if he had not acknowledged them. The psychological component of the interrogation was characterized by repeated accusations that he was an immoral person and a traitor. He was allowed to speak only in response to specific questions directed to him.

Communist authorities recognized the limited value of torture in soliciting information from prisoners. However, if the psychological or moral approach did not work, the interrogators would adopt physical means of coercion. During this phase of the interrogation, the accused was made uncomfortable and seated on a hard chair, preferably sitting on the edge. He was made to sit up straight and not support himself in any way. He was not allowed to move and at times he was required to stand, again without supporting himself in any way. Toilet breaks were infrequent and only given in an emergency. In numerous documents, communist interrogators cited specific targets for physical abuse. Some of those were bare hands, hitting the bridge of the nose with a rubber truncheon, shoulder joints, the soles of bare feet, and finger tips. Pulling the subject's hair was another method of torture. Hair would be burned from the top of the head, chest, or crotch. Other methods included using cigarettes to burn the areas around the prisoner's eyes and mouth, placing a pencil between the fingers and then crushing them, requiring prisoners to stand at attention with arms in the air for several hours, and removing the windows from the prisoner's cell in cold weather. On various occasions guards would falsely inform prisoners that their loved ones had died. Mock executions were another tactic that was employed to destroy a prisoner's mental well-being.

After two days of continuous torture, the accused might be given tea and a piece of bread so he would be able to continue the interrogation. If the prisoner collapsed and could not be revived, the authorities would have lost. However, if he finally began to give information, he could receive nutritious food. At this point, the prisoner was required to write a new statement confessing his anti-state activities.

Nevertheless, the leaders of the agencies undertaking torture did see certain values in these procedures. The targets of this brutality were not simply the people subjected to torture but, more importantly, other people who were still at large and resisting the government. It also served as part of a process of re-education by reshaping the victims' perceptions. Afterward, if they survived physically, they would be more pliable and likely to support the regime. If a show trial was the final step in this process, as the accused, one after the other, make the same statements of self-degradation, citizens who observed the trials would eventually think that at least some of these people must be telling the truth. In addition, once the accused had made his public statement, there was no opportunity for a retraction or to take back the names of other people that had been implicated. Eventually, this entire show was intended not only to secure information and confessions, but also to shape popular attitudes by stimulating fear.

Another communist interrogation system that borrowed heavily from the Soviet model but incorporated certain traditional elements was that of Romania in the years just after World War II. The case of an individual identified as "Samuel Feld" illustrates features of the interrogation system of communist Romania. Feld had an eleven year career in Romania's Ministry of Internal Affairs. He had served as chief of the counterespionage and interrogation services for his region near Brasov. His interrogation file cited numerous but imprecise "grave transgressions." According to his file, he had failed to denounce crimes, had joined the secret police under false pretexts, failed to respect the working class, had connections with Zionists, and had relatives who lived abroad. Educational standards of personnel in the security services were extremely low during this period. In comparison with most of his colleagues, Feld was highly intelligent and behaved in a superior manner. Combined with his Jewish background, these characteristics contributed to his unpopularity and, in 1954, to an investigation that aimed at his expulsion from the Ministry.

What is most apparent about the way in which the Romanian investigators attempted to discern the truth was that they had an agenda with required outcomes. Because mere facts were not the most important things, once a person became an official suspect, there was little chance that the interrogators would fail to get the answers they needed for a conviction. Guilt could be assumed on the basis of class or ethnic considerations. His personal identity mattered more than what he might have actually done or not done. A significant fact in Feld's case was that he was Jewish. Since he was being investigated during a time of anti-Semitism in Romania, many witnesses referenced this factor.

While there is no record that Feld was subjected to torture, he did have to endure an investigation that ran for eight years. Considering that he had only served in the Ministry of Internal Affairs that seems excessive. A basic part of his investigation was a requirement that he prepare a full written account of his life. This was a common require-ment even for people not being investigated but should a person attract the attention of security personnel, his "autobiography" was always an element of the investigation. Feld was periodically required to re-write his autobiography and the different versions were always scrutinized in an effort to catch inconsistencies. For example, much was made of his inconsistent statements about his desire for higher education. At some points he had dreamed of being a doctor and later it was a dream of becoming a lawyer.

At the end of this eight year ordeal, Feld was dismissed from the Ministry and had to return all of the medals he had received for exemplary service. He also lost his membership in the Romanian Communist Party. He did not, however, face imprisonment and after a decade of requesting to leave Romania, he was finally allowed to immigrate to West Germany.

When looking at brutal methods of interrogations, we naturally think about the Nazis, the Soviets, the Chinese, and other similar states. However, they are not alone in this category, and democratic states are often guilty of the same behavior, even though there may be legal and political consequences. As the victors in World War II, the British were better able to keep unpleasant and illegal details of their interrogations away from the eyes of the British public. It was only in recent years that more information has emerged. There were investigations and several officers had to face a court martial on charges of torture. Their defense was that they were following orders and the most prominent defendants were acquitted. The fact that the very survival of the United Kingdom was at stake added to an atmosphere of relatively lenient prosecutions.

The secret interrogation center that has received most of the attention was known as the London Cage and was one of a network of nine secret sites operated in Britain. These nine facilities were benignly run and were operated by the Prisoner of War Interrogation Section while the Directorate of Military Intelligence had overall responsibility. As a transit camp, the London Cage should have been on the Red Cross list, but no information about Germans detained at the London Cage was shared with the Red Cross. Officially, this facility did not exist. Prisoners who resisted all interrogation efforts at Britain's other centers and were seen as high value were generally sent to the London Cage. It was the subject of a book by that name which was first published in 1957 and was heavily censored. A more complete account appeared in 2017. The Germans who passed through the London Cage were beaten, forced to assume stress positions for days at a time, and were deprived of sleep. Guards jokingly referred to themselves as the English Gestapo and threatened prisoners with unnecessary surgery carried out by people with no medical qualifications. They also told prisoners that they would be killed and buried in unmarked graves.

There was another nearby secret facility used to extract military information from German prisoners at a time when there was a real fear that the Germans would invade England. The facility was at nearby Latchmere House and known by the code name Camp 020. It was managed by Lieutenant Colonel Robin Stephens who gained notoriety for his work in Germany after the war ended. It enjoyed the services of one full time medical officer, a psychiatrist who helped devise torture techniques that would leave no marks while breaking the will of the prisoners. Colonel Stephens informed his officers that their guideline was "truth in the shortest possible time" by using unspecified "special methods." Starvation and sensory deprivation

were known to be among the techniques used in Camp 020. For especially recalcitrant prisoners, he had constructed a punishment room
known as Cell 13. During its time in operation, approximately five
hundred German prisoners were processed at Camp 020. In addition,
this facility was used for interrogating members of the British Union of
Fascists who were seen as a possible fifth column for the German army
should it invade.

The man who operated the London Cage was Colonel Alexander
Scotland, a nephew of the famous playwright George Bernard Shaw,
who prided himself for being able to get information out of any of his
prisoners. He was observed using a "truth serum" during an interrogation of a prisoner. After the war, numerous allegations were made
against operations at the London Cage. There were accusations that
torture and psychological abuse were common. Prisoners were said
to have been beaten, kicked, and subjected to an electric device
in an effort to force confessions. Prisoners were warned that if they
did not cooperate, they could vanish without a trace. In 1946, the
International Red Cross requested permission to visit the London
Cage but were barred from doing so.

Because of Scotland's pride in his professionalism, in the 1950s he
wanted to publish his memoirs explaining his successes and his use
of unorthodox methods of interrogations. In his manuscript Scotland
acknowledged that his brutal methods continued after the war. When
he submitted his manuscript for official approval, authorities were
fearful of the damage his work might cause. All four typed copies were
confiscated by Special Branch officers and any person who knew of its
contents was threatened with prosecution under the Official Secrets
Act. Even Colonel Scotland was threatened with arrest. Fearful that
the manuscript might be published in the United States, authorities
made a deal under which a heavily redacted version of the book could
be published in 1957. Approximately half the manuscript was deleted,
including all references to interrogation methods, specific prisoners, or
the use of drugs and torture. In its final version, there was no indication of what life had been like in the London Cage. When the official
files were sent to the National Archives, large sections were missing.

The Ministry of Defense said the documents had been damaged by flood water and asbestos.

In occupied Germany, people seen as a threat to the Allied occupation could be taken to Bad Nenndorf, which had been a famous German spa town. Lieutenant Colonel Robin Stephens, who operated Camp 020 in London, also ran the Bad Nenndorf facility while being permanently assigned to MI5. Stephens was an authoritarian xenophobic individual who directed his 20 interrogators to use whatever skills were required to break a prisoner. In spite of that determination, Stephens was emphatic in his rejection of torture, insisting that it was ineffective. Of the 20 interrogators, there were 12 British from various UK services. Many were skilled linguists who were proficient in communicating in any German dialect. Most of the remaining interrogators were German Jewish refugees who had joined the Allies in 1939 or 1940.

Bad Nenndorf was intended to be used to interrogate former Nazis and help the Allies defend against the so-called "Werewolves" that had pledged to initiate guerrilla warfare in post-war Germany. It later targeted people spying for the Soviet Union and held an assortment of Germans, Russians, Czechs and Hungarians.

The guards at Bad Nenndorf were mostly young soldiers with at least a year of combat experience and many of them had helped to liberate Belsen. As you would expect after what they had seen at Belsen, they felt the Germans deserved no mercy. The selection process for the guard force tended to draw from the ranks of British soldiers facing disciplinary action for their violence. These guards were expected to enforce the "discipline" necessary to break prisoners both mentally and physically. This was an important part of the Bad Nenndorf interrogation process. Prisoners were on a starvation diet and were awakened throughout the night. They would often be required to walk in their cells from early morning until late at night. Guards used thumbscrews and "shin screws" as tools to weaken their prisoners. Selected prisoners received even more severe treatment as guards were instructed to subject them to physical beatings that would make them more pliant during their long interrogations.

The interrogations often included threats to arrest the prisoners' wives and children, to torture, and even murder them. Bad Nenndorf authorities justified these threats by saying that they were never carried out. Prisoners who were seen as uncooperative during their interrogations were often sent to a punishment cell where they would be stripped naked and buckets of cold water would be thrown on them. This process could last for weeks, even during the most severe cold weather. Naked prisoners could be hand-cuffed back to back and forced to stand before open windows during the winter. One prisoner, an anti-Nazi who had been tortured by the Gestapo, said Bad Nenndorf was worse than any Nazi camp in which he had stayed. Another prisoner claimed he had been hanged by his wrists during interrogations and that his finger nails had been torn out.

Over a period of twenty two months, more than four hundred detainees were interrogated at Bad Nenndorf. In January and February of 1947, prisoners were taken to a civilian hospital near Bremen. When the doctors examined the Bad Nenndorf prisoners they noted the abuse to which they had been subjected. The doctors complained that it was obvious prisoners had routinely been beaten, frozen, and deprived of sleep. All of them were near starvation and two of them died in the hospital.

Some Bad Nenndorf accounts, such as the death of a former SS officer, are bizarre. The officer had been severely beaten when he was arrested in January 1947 and by the time he arrived at the camp, he could not be interrogated because he had lost consciousness. When he died a few days later, camp officials did not acknowledge who he was. Instead, they informed grave diggers that he was a British officer who had died of an infectious disease. His body was sewn into a blanket, placed into a grave, and covered with quicklime. He was buried with full military honors and the cross over his grave had an English name. The curious question is why was this man's death and identity hidden? Much later, when Foreign Office declassified papers about this incident, it was revealed that the German was actually working as a spy for the Americans and providing information about former Nazi officers. By itself, that would not have been shocking but what did stun researchers was learning that the man had served in Poland, was wanted by the Polish government as a war criminal, and that his crimes were known by the Americans. To this day, his grave is still marked by a tombstone with a false British name meaning that even in death, this war criminal eluded pursuers.

Residents of Bad Nenndorf were bitter about British behavior when their forces arrived to take over from the easy-going American infantry that had first occupied the town. They were given ninety minutes to pack and leave the town. Barbed wire fences were hurriedly erected as the town center was transformed into a prison camp. The bath house was taken over and the cubicles were taken out. Heavy steel doors were installed as the cubicles were turned each into cells. Prisoners were brought in by trucks and cattle cars. Locals often claimed that during the night, if you crept close to the wire, you could hear screams. Others maintained that during the day there was an eerie silence and people were never seen. Because of Bad Nenndorf's reputation, Germans referred to it as "das verboten dorf," the forbidden village.

The report by a British court of inquiry concluded that the complaints against Bad Nenndorf were valid and made it obvious that even the London Cage was not as bad as this facility. Prisoners had been tortured with devices recovered from a Gestapo prison in Hamburg. Colonel Stephens and two other officers had to face courts martial because UK authorities considered the charges to be credible. Stephens was acquitted and one of the officers was found guilty of neglecting the prisoners and was forced to leave the service. In short, the punishments were modest. A more compelling motive for the British government was to prevent the public and especially the Soviets from learning about what happened at Bad Nenndorf. The camp was closed in July 1947 and all of the barbed wire was removed. The cells were taken out of the bath house and it was restored as a facility for elderly German retirees.

British Interrogation Successes

I T WOULD BE A MISTAKE TO associate British interrogation methods with the unsavory activities at the London Cage and Bad Nenndorf. Studies of the UK's Naval Intelligence Division (NID) provide instruction on effective methods relevant to World War II as well as the contemporary era. The NID was involved in the only undertaking that lasted for the entire war and had both tactical and strategic relevance—*the U-boat struggle*. Their success in this effort was instrumental in changing POW interrogation from an incidental source of information into a vital part of the British intelligence collection effort. This work was centered at two country estates— Latimer House and Wilton Park. The small team was known as the Combined Services Detailed Interrogation Centre (CSDIC) and consisted largely of reservists. Their work began with three officers and one civilian assistant in December 1940. By the end of the war there were thirteen Naval and Marine officers.

The work of CSDIC was greatly advanced by the capture of the largely undamaged German submarine U-570 on 27 August 1941. The German crew was rescued by the British as the submarine was hauled to a British naval facility for examination. There were no reports about the British capture of the vessel or the survival of crew members who were sent to POW camps in the Bahamas. From that point on, the CSDIC, which consisted of non-naval personnel, was required to develop an intimate knowledge of the vessel that had been home to the captured Germans. This familiarity was essential in helping interrogators assess the truthfulness of information provided by the submariners.

In developing their strategies, the CSDIC rejected torture, as well as the use of drugs. The Naval Intelligence Division experimented with drugs early in the war and determined that they were unreliable. Torture was explicitly rejected, not on moral grounds, but because British authorities feared it would justify greater German use of torture against Allied POWs.

At Latimer House, there were three basic tools used in gathering information. The first was direct interrogation. For this to be effective, interrogators had to establish themselves as authoritative on all matters and they needed to carry the correct military rank. Because the Germans placed great importance on rank, interrogators had access to an assortment of uniform jackets displaying appropriate insignia for rank and military specialization. This helped interrogators in establishing a convincing bluff.

One useful effect of direct interrogation was that it raised specific topics. Even if the Germans gave no valid information during the interrogation itself, there was a good prospect that upon returning to their cells, they might boast about how they had deceived the British. The second basic tool used at Latimer House was covert listening through hidden microphones. By recording conversations the Germans thought were confidential, the British gained insight and information about the topics raised during direct interrogation. The CSDIC staff provided prisoners with newspapers that were another source of stimulation for conversations among the Germans. As a result of these tactics, the Germans came to see their captors as all-knowing people whom they could not deceive.

A third basic tool was the use of informants placed in the cells with the submariners. The informants were drawn from the ranks of 93 anti-Nazi German refugees who had volunteered to help British intelligence. Four refugees were selected and provided with the information to convince the prisoners that they were also submariners that had fallen into the hands of CSDIC. Eventually these four were supplemented with genuine German servicemen who had decided to help the British. From that time on, the informant system gained efficacy. None of the informants knew about the secret microphones, a situation that provided another check for the British to be sure of the honesty of their sources.

The Latimer House work helped POW interrogation evolve from something of occasional value to an important weapon in the U-boat war. The British learned that (1) the U-boat dive capabilities exceeded the distance covered by British depth charges, that (2) the Germans had broken the British convoy code, and that (3) some German destroyers carried six-inch guns. By listening to German conversations, CSDIC was able to provide valuable assistance to British psychological warfare operations by assessing the impacts of myriad themes. With this information, the BBC could offer information in its broadcasts that made it appear that the Allies had well-placed spies within the German military. Each broadcast of this type helped spark a renewed spy hysteria in Germany. The British work went well beyond being simply a search for truth.

Technology and Interrogation

THERE HAS ALWAYS BEEN CONSIDERABLE APPEAL in the idea that a machine, something not restricted by sentiment or prejudice and devoid of human frailties, could distinguish between truth and lies. In pursuit of this laudable objective, countless scientists and innovators have endeavored to create the perfect technology to do this. Not only would such technology provide relief for overworked investigators, it would guarantee a perfect result.

Technology assisted interrogation was developed on the basis of a metabolic study at the Mayo Clinic. This technology was first used by police in Gwinnet County, Georgia where the police placed a thermal imagery camera behind a panel close to the interview subject. The highly sensitive camera measures small changes in temperature while the camera operator notes the questions that elicited these changes. The question techniques used by the police officers reflect their dependence on this technology to help detect deceptive responses.

As noted above, technology like thermal imagery cameras plays an important role during interrogation. The polygraph is an even more advanced technology aid and is commonly used, but not regarded as being absolutely reliable. One of the most significant problems with such advanced technology is that it leads to an assumption that a technological device can be a substitute for serious interrogations and detailed investigative work.

One of the more valuable technological innovations is biometrics. Experts who rely on this technology often boast that the "eyes don't lie." Iris scans, coupled with fingerprints, closed-circuit TV surveillance, and facial images have created tremendous challenges for terrorists and other criminal types to cross borders, pass through airports, or penetrate denied areas. Unfortunately, these technologies create difficulties for law enforcement personnel who are working against terrorists. The erosion of anonymity in this age of sophisticated technology has limited physical mobility and put limits on clandestine operations. In response to this situation, in 2016 the Central Intelligence Agency created the Directorate of Digital Innovation which examines the full range of digital concerns from cybersecurity to IT infrastructure. This innovation was necessary because, as the Agency acknowledged, some of its most important components were hampered by their lack of digital skills. It was also necessitated because biometrics technologies were being used by criminal and terrorist organizations and gave US adversaries the ability to track and identify Western intelligence officers. When Israeli agents carried out the 2010 assassination of terrorist leader Mahmoud al-Mabhouh, for example, Hamas investigators were able to identify 27 Israeli agents who worked on this operation.

As mentioned earlier, undercover officers provide a valuable supplement to the interrogation process by gathering information outside the interrogation room. It is a deceptive tactic but is effective in collecting information to help solve a crime. The interrogation in and of itself is not the most important step in solving a case. What matters most is simply gathering all of the information that relates to the crime. As governments utilize modern technology to keep track of citizens, we are learning that this knowledge in the hands of authorities, coupled with a lack of transparency, undermines the ability to have secrets.

One of the many by-products of the COVID pandemic is official efforts to create a vaccine passport. The amount of personal information carried on such a proposed digital device is enormous. Although we don't yet know exactly how such a device will be configured, or even if it will come into existence, personal privacy is already increasingly elusive. What this means is that many of the questions that will be directed at a suspect are already answered and the interrogator/suspect interactions are less crucial to solving a case. This should not, however, suggest that investigators should ignore the necessary characteristics required of an effective interrogator.

The Polygraph

WIDELY PRAISED IN BOTH TELEVISION PROGRAMS as well as police publications, the polygraph was invented in 1921 by a medical student at the University of California, Berkeley, John Augustus Larson, who was working with a Berkeley police officer. There were several pivotal years in the development of the polygraph: 1895, 1904, and 1906, most notably. Most of these innovations were rudimentary but were far more sophisticated than those of the Middle Ages that involved the use of boiling water on the assumption that honest men could endure this better than liars.

In 1906, William Moulton Marston, who was working with German prisoners of war, created a machine that relied on fluctuations of systolic blood pressure to prove when a person was lying. The project was canceled due to poor test results. Marston continued his efforts and at one point credited his wife Elizabeth with providing inspiration for his work on deception research. Marston consistently referred to himself as the "father of the polygraph." Always a self-promoter, Marston even appeared in an advertisement for the Gillette razor company claiming that the polygraph proved that Gillette razors were better than those of their competition although it is hard to imagine how this was possible.

Larson's demeanor was more serious and his device measured blood pressure and breathing. Larson claimed that together they would indicate if a respondent was being deceptive. It was further developed by a Larson colleague and then by interrogation specialist John E. Reid. A major step in the general acceptance of the polygraph occurred when the FBI purchased it and it emerged as a $2 billion industry complete with a lobbyist promoting its use. The polygraph test emerged as the "gold standard" for determining if a suspect was being deceptive.

The operational principle of the modern polygraph machine—often known as a lie detector—is that it measures specific physiological indicators. These would include physiological indicators such as blood pressure, pulse rate, respiration, skin conductivity and other indicators that might distinguish a deceptive response. The polygraph is used in the interrogation of criminal suspects, as well as in the screening of applicants for positions in sensitive organizations and positions. Officials within the US government are not likely to use the term lie detector and prefer the much more elaborate term "psychophysiological detection of deception." This technical designation is less ambitious than the somewhat misleading term "lie detector."

Studies by the National Academy of Sciences have raised questions about the value of the polygraph, leading operators to devise various methods to improve the credibility of the device. Polygraph supporters have made much of the control question test which is supposed to provide a base line for a person deliberately telling a lie. If the subject of the exam claims to have kidnapped the Lindberg baby, his physiological indicators will reflect an anomaly. Therefore, should he tell a lie about whether he has disclosed classified information to a person not authorized to have that information, his physiological indicators will reveal his lie. The sad truth is that this is not always the case. People who have a conscience and a sense of personal responsibility are more likely to produce indications often associated with deception. Examiners often remark that devoutly religious people like Catholics and Baptists are more likely to fail the exam. Even runners whose heart rates are normally slower will have problems because their heart rate is too consistent for the machine to show significant variations. However, a psychopathic person who has no sense of guilt is more likely to go through the exam and display no physiological indicators of deception. There are also counter measures that can be used in order to defeat the polygraph technology.

Over the years, the polygraph has been viewed as biased against the innocent and has become increasingly controversial as questions have been raised about its accuracy. The relative ease with which traitor Aldrich Ames got past the polygraph is a good indication of the short-comings of the technology underlying the machine. Between 1986 and 1991, while actively spying for the USSR, Ames survived two poly-graph exams. Another person who inexplicably passed two polygraph exams was serial killer Charles Edmund Cullen. Cullen had worked on cardiac wards administering drugs on a regular basis and apparently had no feelings of guilt about his killings. Larry Wu-tai Chin, who was a CIA employee spying for the Peoples Republic of China, got past the polygraph on two occasions. He explained his success by saying the questions were vague and in English rather than his native Chinese. He said that had the questions been in Chinese, he could not have defeated the machine. An employee of the Defense Intelligence Agency, Ana Belen Montes, was a spy for Cuba who had no trouble with the polygraph and was highly regarded within the DIA. She was exposed thanks to the efforts of one individual who caught her lying about why she stepped out of a high level Pentagon meeting. Another CIA employee, Karl Koecher, worked in the Agency for 19 years while supplying sensitive information to the KGB. A CIA-administered polygraph did not detect Koecher's deceptive responses. Koecher was arrested by the FBI when he and his wife attempted to flee the United States. Their flight was prompted not by fear of the polygraph but by the defection of a senior Polish official who knew about them. A final high level spy whose perfidy was not detected by his polygraph exam was an FBI intelligence analyst named Leandro Aragoncillo. He had been assigned to the White House working for Vice President Al Gore and later for Vice President Dick Cheney.

In 1984, the so-called Green River Killer, Gary Ridgway, got past a polygraph test while another suspect failed the test. With this, atten-tion was directed away from Ridgway. However, twenty years later, when DNA evidence again pointed to Ridgway, he confessed. In the years since 1984, he had killed seven more women. Critics observed that the polygraph test was a factor in these deaths.

It can be equally bad when a polygraph indicates a suspect was deceptive in spite of his innocence, and the suspect lives under suspicion because no one else is apprehended. In 1986, a man named Bill Wegerle faced suspicion when his wife was murdered. The police administered a polygraph and he hired a company to give him a second test. Both indicated that he was being deceptive but since there was no physical evidence linking him to the crime, he was never arrested. Although many people suspected him, it was not until 2005 when evidence connected her death with serial killer Dennis Rader, known as the "BTK Killer" for "bind, torture, kill," that the husband was finally cleared.

There are also occasions when a suspect is subjected to prolonged polygraph testing and, upon being told he failed, has agreed to confess. This happened in the case of former FBI Agent Richard Miller who had been charged with espionage. He maintained his innocence but was convinced he was certain to be convicted because of the extended presentation of polygraph results to an increasingly skeptical jury. He felt he had no option but to confess. However, his conviction was overturned by a judge who maintained that the "full prejudicial impact" of the polygraph results meant he had not received a fair trial.

Even though polygraph results are of limited judicial value in criminal cases, they are still used by government agencies to screen possible employees and to investigate possible security breaches. There are two possible issues in this regard. First, there is the suggestion that the polygraph is useful in detecting espionage. The second is the possibility that when employees fear the polygraph, they may be less likely to engage in espionage. This is regarded as the most likely use of the polygraph. US Navy spy Jonathan Pollard was warned by his Israeli handlers that he should resign if he knew he was going to be subjected to a polygraph examination.

Several notorious spies have ignored the polygraph threat, despite the fact that their handlers seemed very sensitive to this concern. Like Pollard, the longtime Navy spy John Anthony Walker was cautioned to avoid the polygraph and not engage in espionage until he had been promoted to the highest position not requiring the polygraph. They also discouraged his recruitment of family members, advice that he consistently ignored. His decision to deliver secrets to the Soviet

Union was motivated by financial need. He had invested all of his savings in land in South Carolina that he used to open an unsuccessful bar. Deciding that espionage might be a way out, in 1967 Walker went into the Soviet Embassy in Washington and handed the security officer a bag of secret documents to show what he could deliver. The Soviets were convinced of their validity and selected the prominent KGB officer Oleg Kalugin to manage his America-based work. Kalugin drove around Washington selecting the dead drops that Walker would use for deliveries. Walker's downfall had little to do with routine counter-espionage protocols, polygraphs, or even poor tradecraft. There was never an indication that any security service had detected Walker's ambitious operations. At one point, he forged papers showing his security clearance had been renewed, a brazen action that should have been spotted. Many observers later commented that Walker was a beneficiary of dumb luck and shoddy counterintelligence operations.

In the end, marital tensions and his angry ex-wife Barbara undermined what had become, for the Navy, an extremely destructive operation and for Walker a very profitable family and friend-based operation. By retiring from the Navy in 1975 and divorcing his wife, Walker was free to travel to meet the friends and family members who supplied him with sensitive documents about Navy communications procedures. When he tried to recruit his daughter to spy for him, Walker's ex-wife called the FBI and told an agent about his activities. Because she was drunk when the agent visited her, her account lacked credibility and was not immediately acted upon. Walker's daughter added to his ex-wife's report but, like her mother, her intense bitterness diminished her credibility. Eventually, the FBI organized a search of the Walker home that revealed an abundance of evidence. Faced with this, Walker, in exchange for a promise not to pursue the death penalty, agreed to make a confession.

An equally destructive spy for the Soviet Union, Robert Hanssen, was never deterred from committing espionage by the threat of a polygraph exam. In fact, during the 25 years that Hanssen was in the FBI, he was never required to take a polygraph. In discussing this after his conviction, Hanssen declared that he felt the threat of a polygraph would have given him second thoughts about becoming a spy. His primary motivation for espionage seemed to have been his arrogance, resentment over not being promoted to a higher position, and a belief that he could fool those who outranked him within the FBI. He did not ask for much money and gave away most of what he got from the Soviets.

The overall record of the polygraph as a deterrent to espionage is not encouraging. In the post-World War II era, there are six Americans who were required to submit to a polygraph examination during the time they were engaging in espionage. None of them was tripped up by the process. In fact, Cuban spy Ana Belen Montes, who had worked for the Defense Intelligence Agency (DIA) for many years, took a counterintelligence full-scope polygraph in 1994. There were no indications of deception during the exam. Undeterred by such embarrassments, in 2008 DIA expanded its polygraph testing program. Under this policy, all prospective DIA employees would be tested and current employees would be required to take the polygraph exam at least once every year. For all counterintelligence testing, DIA uses the computerized Lafayette polygraph system, which is notorious for its technical flaws. In spite of serious questions about the utility of polygraph results, the system enjoys considerable support within the bureaucracy.

One of the many shortcomings of the polygraph is that the operator is often likely to try to trick a subject into saying something that might constitute an admission of being deceptive. He may ask a subject what it was about a certain question that bothered him. He will offer the subject a chance to clarify any uncertainty about his response. Another common tactic for soliciting an incriminating admission is to ask what a subject was thinking about when he answered a particular question. This is generally a bluff that will affect his assessment of a subject's performance. The subject should never elaborate beyond the specifics of the question asked.

After almost a century of work with the polygraph, there has been a continuing skeptical attitude and most courts are hesitant about accepting results of a polygraph examination. Research conducted by scientific institutes usually describes the polygraph as an inaccurate tool that can be defeated by countermeasures. Enthusiastic advocates of the polygraph maintain that its results are valid in 90% of the cases in which it is employed. The National Research Council disputes these claims and argues that while the device can measure physiological reactions, it cannot discern the reasons for those reactions. Like a person entering the dentist's office, the subject of a polygraph examination is going to be nervous and display a variety of reactions in response to an event. Those reactions could have a tremendous impact on his career. Everybody entering the CIA headquarters building is greeted by a sign proclaiming that your entry constitutes agreement to undergo a search. That includes, presumably, a polygraph exam. Do you trust it? Should it trust you?

Is the Search for Truth a Fair Process?

IN SEARCHING FOR TRUTH, OUR SOCIETY has worked to eliminate torture and to exclude coerced confessions in criminal matters. Yet the interrogation process is intended to manipulate the suspect into confessing. We are certainly concerned about the fairness and morality of interrogations but there is a legitimate concern about whether this process can ever be fair. If you find yourself in a detained interrogation, this means you are a target and the police intend to charge you. In their effort to gain a confession, the police will exploit human weaknesses wherever they can be found.

Police dramas will often portray the suspect as a cunning evil person who has a massive supply of illegal cash to pay for his devious attorneys. It is more likely that the suspect will be a fearful person who lacks the cunning and resources to defeat a team of police officers who have experience as well as information about the suspect and the crime of which he is suspected. What this means is that when the police interrogate the average suspect, it is not a fair fight. At the end of the day, police officers generally go home. If they were able to develop probable cause for an arrest, the suspect would remain in custody.

The police interrogation will proceed on an assumption that you are guilty until you can convince the police otherwise. The interrogators are likely to filter out exculpatory information that might constitute evidence of your innocence of the crime. After all, they are evaluated on the basis of their conviction rate, so they need for you to be guilty. Although a forced confession will be rejected by the court, there is always a subtle element of coercion involved, and police will imply, but not promise, that you will receive lenient treatment if you quickly confess and save everybody's time. The psychological aspects of an interrogation have many of the attributes of "brain washing" in which the suspect is pressured to acknowledge his guilt.

The brainwashing process works to create insecurity, confusion, and discomfort in an effort to break its subjects. This process involves the use of several techniques that are also routinely used in police interrogations. One technique is for the interrogator to move in and out of the personal space of the suspect. This forces the suspect into a position of feeling small and vulnerable. During this time, the suspect is not allowed to speak so he cannot begin to mount any sort of self-defense. He is informed that his time to speak will come later. The interrogator will develop a narrative in which there are contrasting views about why—not if—he committed the crime that is being investigated. One view is something that may be regrettable and can be more or less understood. It does not require the suspect to admit that he is evil. The second view is that he committed the crime for the base motives that are beyond the realm of civilized behavior. Accepting the first view gives the suspect a modest degree of dignity and self-respect. He is a normal person who has made a mistake and nothing more. In presenting the contrasting views, the interrogator has given the suspect a way out of his difficult situation, thus bringing this part of his ordeal to an end.

The police have an advantage in that they can employ tactics that are misleading to the suspect's interest but are nonetheless legal. One example is that the police may say that while this is an open and shut case, they need something to take to the district attorney. The truth is that if the case is already open and shut, the police don't need anything from the suspect. They can proceed to the next stage without any other statement. The suspect, if he believes this is a time to give his side of the story, may well say something that will corroborate evidence the police already possess. This statement will constitute a confession and will undermine a defendant's case. The only way in which this statement can be thrown out is if the police continued the interrogation after a suspect had requested his right to an attorney. The danger to the suspect at this point is that the police are often able to trick a suspect into reinitiating the interrogation. A casual invitation to add a few words to his previous statements can often be sufficient for the suspect to start talking again.

Another ploy is the suggestion by the police that this is a friendly conversation and they simply want to know what happened. Once this is accomplished, the police will suggest that you will be free to go home. The truth is that if you are being detained in an interrogation room, you are the target of the investigation and once the police develop probable cause to arrest you, you will not be going home.

One way in which the suspect might avoid this trap is to make a firm statement proclaiming his innocence at the start of the interrogation. If the suspect has a reliable defense attorney, he is likely to do this. This action is preferable to the situation in which the suspect refuses to say anything at all.

Interrogation is simply one of several avenues in pursuit of the truth. In recent years technology has been employed as an improved substitute for older, traditional approaches. Forensic science and DNA are prominent and promising alternatives developed by technology. The advent of the modern polygraph after World War II was expected to be the definitive scientific vehicle in searching for the truth. Unfortunately, experience and careful studies have exposed the flaws of this technical innovation. Like the traditional police interrogation, the polygraph examination can be manipulated and productive of false confessions. Even the suspect's confession can be flawed when it is coerced, even when the coercion is psychological rather than physical. Moreover, confessions have sometimes been based on memories that were not genuine but generated by the interrogation process.

Even conventional research can bring disappointments when the official documents, reports, and records are tainted by erroneous data or distorted by deliberate deceptions. The insider lies that have undermined popular faith in our elites have created difficulties for honest researchers hoping to prepare honest accounts of public affairs. More recently, the fact checkers have offered their services as arbiters of the truth. An examination of their methodologies and backgrounds has often brought disappointment. With competing services and contradictory claims, citizens are forced to rely on their own judgements in making important decisions about policies and politicians.

About the Author

JOHN KIRIAKOU IS A FORMER CIA counterterrorism officer, former senior investigator for the Senate Foreign Relations Committee, and former counterterrorism consultant for ABC News. He was responsible for the capture in Pakistan in 2002 of Abu Zubaydah, then believed to be the third-ranking official in al-Qaeda. In 2007, Kiriakou blew the whistle on the CIA's torture program, telling ABC News that the CIA tortured prisoners, that torture was official US government policy, and that the policy had been approved by then-President George W. Bush.

In 2012, Kiriakou was honored with the Joe A. Callaway Award for Civic Courage, an award given to individuals who "advance truth and justice despite the personal risk it creates," and by the inclusion of his portrait in artist Robert Shetterly's series Americans Who Tell the Truth, which features notable truth-tellers throughout American history. Kiriakou won the PEN Center USA's prestigious First Amendment Award in 2015, the first Blueprint International Whistleblowing Prize for Bravery and Integrity in the Public Interest in 2016, and the Sam Adams Award for Integrity in Intelligence, also in 2016. A second portrait, by the noted Chinese artist Ai Weiwei, is in the permanent collection of the Smithsonian Institution.

Kiriakou is the author of multiple books on intelligence and the CIA. He lives with his family in Northern Virginia.